1st edito
signed

£ 60

HAROLD MACMILLAN AND
BRITAIN'S WORLD ROLE

To Ronan —

With best wishes,

R.

1996

Harold Macmillan and Britain's World Role

Edited by

Richard Aldous
Lecturer in Modern British History
University College Dublin

Sabine Lee
Lecturer in German History
University of Birmingham

Introduced by
Sir Robert Rhodes James

First published in Great Britain 1996 by
MACMILLAN PRESS LTD
Houndmills, Basingstoke, Hampshire RG21 6XS
and London
Companies and representatives
throughout the world

A catalogue record for this book is available
from the British Library.

ISBN 0–333–63053–X

 First published in the United States of America 1996 by
ST. MARTIN'S PRESS, INC.,
Scholarly and Reference Division,
175 Fifth Avenue,
New York, N.Y. 10010

ISBN 0–312–12578–X

Library of Congress Cataloging-in-Publication Data
Harold Macmillan and Britain's world role / edited by Richard Aldous
and Sabine Lee ; introduced by Sir Robert Rhodes James.
p.   cm.
Includes bibliographical references and index.
ISBN 0–312–12578–X (cloth)
1. Macmillan, Harold, 1894–1986.   2. Great Britain—Politics and
government—1945–1964.   3. Great Britain—Foreign relations—1945–
4. World politics—1945–   I. Aldous, Richard.   II. Lee, Sabine.
DA566.9.M33H37   1996
941.085—dc20
95–14917
CIP

10   9   8   7   6   5   4   3   2   1
05   04   03   02   01   00   99   98   97   96

Printed in Great Britain by
Ipswich Book Co Ltd, Ipswich, Suffolk

for David Reynolds

Contents

Acknowledgements

The editors would like to thank:

The Centre of International Studies, Cambridge and, in particular, its former director, Mr Richard Langhorne, for encouragement and sponsorship of the 1993 conference *'Staying in the Game': Harold Macmillan and Britain's World Role;* St John's College, Cambridge for hosting the conference; Dr Neville Wylie, Junior Research Fellow at New Hall, Cambridge for his characteristically amusing and efficient assistance in conference organisation; Mr Tim Farmiloe and Ms Annabelle Buckley of Macmillan, Mr and Mrs John Aldous, Miss Kathryn McKeggie and Dr Han Lee for their continual support; and finally, Dr David Reynolds of Christ's College, Cambridge. His intellectual rigour, good humour during 'little local difficulties' and the willingness to take his students seriously has been an inspiration to all the young historians contributing to this volume. It is to him that this book is dedicated with our gratitude and respect.

Notes on the Contributors

Sir Robert Rhodes James was a Clerk in the House of Commons, 1955–64, and Conservative Member of Parliament for Cambridge, 1976–92. He is the biographer of Lord Randolph Churchill, Lord Rosebery, Winston Churchill, Anthony Eden and Bob Boothby. He is a Fellow of Wolfson College, Cambridge, and a former Fellow of All Souls College, Oxford.

Richard Aldous is Lecturer in Modern British History, University College Dublin.

Nigel Ashton is Lecturer in Modern History at the University of Liverpool.

Simon J. Ball is Lecturer in Modern History at the University of Glasgow.

Philip E. Hemming is a postgraduate student at St John's College, Cambridge.

Sabine Lee is Lecturer in German History at the University of Birmingham.

Foreword

This book is the happy result of several intensive sessions on various aspects of Harold Macmillan's foreign policy held in Cambridge during July 1993. Dr Richard Aldous and Dr Sabine Lee were the parents of the project, and the Centre of International Studies, of which I was then Director, acted as godfather and provided a *point d'appui* by including the Macmillan meeting, at which these papers were delivered, in its conference series for 1993. St John's College willingly provided a venue in its Fisher Building and a notably convivial lunch for the participants.

A concentration of research at the point where the 30-year rule has delivered up the archives of a highly significant period is to be expected, and the presence of a notable scholar and potential PhD supervisor is likely to draw that concentration to a particular University. In the study of the history of British foreign policy this has happened at Cambridge twice in 30 years. The first occasion drew graduate students to study the origins of the 1914 war with Professor Sir Harry Hinsley; and their research, together with that of others, resulted in the joint work *British Foreign Policy under Sir Edward Grey* (CUP, 1977). The second has been the work done on the late 1950s and early 1960s by graduate students at Cambridge under the influence of Dr David Reynolds of Christ's College. This book is the result of their research, particularly on Harold Macmillan, completed as the archives were released under the 30-year rule.

The book opens with a personal recollection by Sir Robert Rhodes James which is of great value for the context in which it places what follows. Each of the contributors has then looked at Harold Macmillan and Britain's world role in the context of three questions: what was Harold Macmillan's personal role in setting Britain's foreign policy agenda; how successfully did Harold Macmillan manage Britain's decline;

and how did other foreign policy considerations affect decision-making in each of the areas examined.

The contributors deal with five main areas: Richard Aldous tackles Macmillan and the personal diplomacy involved in summitry. Nigel Ashton uses Anglo-Jordanian relations after the Suez crisis as a case-study of Macmillan's attitude to the Middle East. Simon Ball considers Macmillan's role in British defence policy by looking at the restructuring of the Royal Air Force. The deeply uncomfortable gear-changing in British policy during the period is reflected in contributions by Sabine Lee on Macmillan and European integration and by Philip Hemming on Macmillan and decolonisation. Hovering over all of this and particularly affecting the topics considered by Richard Aldous, Simon Ball and Nigel Ashton, is the issue of the Anglo-American relationship.

Until the disorientating uncertainties of the post-bipolar period of the later 1990s created a new crisis for Britain and yet another discussion of her proper role, both in defence and foreign policy, there were two phases of intense questioning and stress during the second half of the twentieth century. The first was imposed by the need to face the onset of the Cold War while still suffering the consequences of war and paying the costs of surviving until victory in 1945. The second coincided with the period considered in this book. Its landmarks were the collapse of the Suez operation in 1956, the unexpectedly successful creation of the first stages of the European Union under the provisions of the treaty of Rome in 1957, the end of Empire during the 1960s, with the consequential arrival of a new Commonwealth and a Third World, and the changed relationship between the Soviet Union and the USA following the Cuba Crisis. If the undisputed leading figure in British policy during the first of these phases was Ernest Bevin, Macmillan, if not so completely, was the icon of the second. The results of new research on Macmillan and his period are thus of great importance for anyone trying to understand the flow of events and policies affecting Britain's outlook on the external world and the official reaction to its changing face since 1945. Macmillan himself perhaps encapsulated its feeling, though for another purpose. Sir Nicholas Henderson recorded in his diaries that speaking on a last visit to Washington during the interregnum between the Carter and Reagan presidencies, Macmillan had opened by remarking: 'As Adam said to Eve when they were leaving the Garden of Eden; we are living in a time of transition.'

The Centre of International Studies at Cambridge was delighted to play even a small role in facilitating so fascinating and important a contribution to our knowledge of British foreign policy during the twentieth century.

Richard Langhorne
Director, Wilton Park
Foreign and Commonwealth Office

1 Harold Macmillan: An Introduction

Robert Rhodes James

The recent centenary of Harold Macmillan's birth was not greeted with much reverence; indeed, the general themes were hostile, even dismissive, especially from those commentators too young to have been politically active when he was a leading, indeed for a time dominant, British political personality. Some of his surviving colleagues were at best ambiguous about him; others were strongly critical. Neither his own memoirs nor Alastair Horne's official biography answered many of the questions raised by this brilliant, fascinating and controversial man, in his variety of talents and interests reminiscent of Disraeli, who still keeps his mystery.

When I entered the House of Commons in 1955 Churchill had just retired, with deep reluctance, to be replaced by Eden. The stars of his government were Rab Butler and Macmillan, who had succeeded Eden as Foreign Secretary. But Rab was not the dominating Chancellor of the Exchequer that he had been; he was still recovering from the death of his wife, and perhaps the exhaustion of four years at the Treasury was also telling on him. His Autumn Budget of 1955 was, politically, a disaster, and precipitated Eden's December reshuffle, when he moved Butler to the Leadership of the House and appointed Macmillan in his place.

Macmillan was indignant; he had been at the Foreign Office for only a matter of months, and it was a post he had long craved for. Eden neither liked nor trusted him, and in any event wanted to be his own Foreign Secretary – hence the promotion of Selwyn Lloyd. Eden's real problems as Prime Minister began with this disastrous step, and

Macmillan was to play a central role in his downfall. It was his role during the Suez Crisis of the summer and autumn of 1956 that gave him a reputation as a Machiavellian political operator of consummate ruthlessness that he never entirely lost.

As has often been remarked, he was a consummate actor, and it was impossible to anticipate what role he was about to play. He was a superb debater, and a powerful speaker in the Commons or on a public platform. In private he was one of the very best conversationalists I have ever met, ranging from lofty purpose to reminiscence, with an impish humour that was to entrance generations of Oxford students when he was Chancellor, and more importantly, back-benchers in the Smoking Room of the Commons or in one of his many London clubs. On one occasion a group of Brendan Bracken's friends met in his old house in Lord North Street, in the lovely library Brendan had built, for a party in his memory. Then Macmillan rose to say a few words; he had no notes, and unhappily his speech was not recorded. It was moving, witty and eloquent – perhaps only Churchill in his prime could have done it as well. It is now lost, save in the memories of the few who had the privilege of being present.

Macmillan's physical courage had been proved in the nightmare of the Western Front, and his political valour in the terrible 1920s and 1930s, first on economic policy and then against Appeasement. He actually resigned the Party Whip on one occasion; it was said that his speeches were too academic, more like lectures than speeches, but he took good advice from, among others, Lloyd George, and gradually matured his own distinctive style, to the point when he could, and did, taken on Bevan and worst him in debate. But this took time, intense application and the capacity to learn from mistakes.

Then, there was nothing bogus or artificial about his loathing of the poverty and unemployment that gripped his Stockton constituency; in this he had kindred spirits in Bob Boothby, Eden and Duff Cooper, especially the first. Their Keynesian solutions outraged both main parties, Snowden being an even more committed deflationist than Neville Chamberlain; the Conservative press was derisive, often suggesting that these young men were in the wrong party.

Political courage in itself is a rare quality; to maintain it year after year, as Macmillan and Boothby did, was quite exceptional. What was so remarkable about their political alliance, which was to prove enduring, was that Boothby had been the lover of Macmillan's wife, Lady Dorothy, since the early 1930s, and was to remain so until her death.

This deeply unhappy story seems to have sharpened Macmillan's political ambitions, and given him a new hardness and purpose. His private life became tragic for himself and his children, most of whom had inherited the 'Cavendish disease', acute alcoholism; the fraught atmosphere at Birch Grove cannot have helped.

It was the war that gave him his opportunity, first as a junior minister and then with a semi-independent role in North Africa that brought out his supreme negotiating and diplomatic skills with the Free French and the Americans. It also brought out an ambition that had not been noticed before by his colleagues. He had become, and was always to remain, a committed professional politician, with his eye on the main chance. His antipathy with Eden increased, but although Churchill distrusted his ambition, he was impressed. His rise had begun.

His conduct during Suez – 'first in, first out' in Harold Wilson's memorable (and true) phrase – was brilliantly concealed. Indeed, it was the hapless Butler who had to bear the brunt of Conservative anger and shock when the operation was stopped; it was not realised for some time that it had been Macmillan more than any other member of the Cabinet who had stopped it with figures of reserves pouring out of the country that were wildly exaggerated. Did Macmillan know that they were? Did he use his position as Chancellor of the Exchequer to destroy Eden? Eden certainly thought so, but his health was temporarily broken, and his position beyond redemption.

Although I was very young and politically inexperienced, it was obvious to me that Butler's position had been fatally eroded, while Macmillan's strong self-confidence increasingly appealed to the utterly demoralised Tory Party. His friends reminded everyone that Rab had been 'a man of Munich', whereas Macmillan had opposed it, thereby casting Rab in the role of an Appeaser. It was tough stuff, and unfair, but it was deadly effective. When Eden had to resign in January 1957 it seemed to me clear that Macmillan would succeed, although not to the political commentators – with the exception of Randolph Churchill, who had exceptional sources of information. Eden had wanted Butler to succeed him, and had expected him to do so, but Macmillan was overwhelmingly the choice of the Cabinet and the Parliamentary Party.

The position of the government was dire. The Party had been emotionally shattered by Suez; the Anglo-American alliance was in tatters; the Commonwealth had endured its greatest strain; and the Russian suppression of the Hungarian uprising had increased East–West tensions to a perilous degree, while the Israelis, forced back to their own boundaries after their victorious charge across the Sinai, accused the British of perfidy. Everywhere one looked, the prospects were grim. Under these sombre shadows, and with Macmillan himself giving his government only a few weeks to live, he became Prime Minister.

How he restored the situation at home and abroad is one of the epics of modern British politics. First with his old friend Eisenhower, and then, much more improbably, with John F. Kennedy, he fully repaired the Anglo-American alliance. His Commonwealth tour was a genuine personal and political triumph, and was perceived as such. He lost his entire Treasury team, but shrugged it off – or appeared to do so – with calm insouciance, as if he had lost a troublesome cook and two kitchen maids. He talked up the greatly improving economy. He began the acceleration of the decolonisation process, particularly in Africa, and took the first steps towards 'doing a de Gaulle' over Cyprus. It was the golden period of Supermac. Everyone cheered up. The Conservatives won the 1959 General Election with surprising ease. And then everything began to go seriously wrong.

One factor was Macmillan's style and personality. In spite of his enjoyment of men's clubs and apparent gregariousness he was in reality a lonely man, and a far more sensitive one than was usually realised. When things began to go wrong, his buoyancy seemed to fade. A series of poor by-election results and other misfortunes in 1962 precipitated his dismissal of seven Cabinet Ministers and a quantity of others ministers in one disastrous fell swoop in July. It was this, rather than Profumo and other later débâcles – and particularly the de Gaulle veto on the British application to join the EEC – that effectively finished his personal authority. The legend of 'unflappability' propagated by Quintin Hailsham now appeared to be just that. The rest was aftermath.

It was to prove a long and largely sad one. The deaths of his wife and two of his children were deep blows, as was that of his devoted friend and supporter John Wyndham, one of the funniest of companions, at too early an age. Gradually his sight faded, the worst of all fates for a compulsive reader. He published his memoirs and diaries, and returned to publishing, but it was the perceived decline of his reputation that was especially hurtful for a proud man who had, after all, devoted his adult life to the service of his country in war and peace.

But then there was the final appearance as the Earl of Stockton, holding the House of Lords and a huge television audience enthralled by the old skills. His speeches now had to be rehearsed totally, and it was while I was lunching with him and Maurice's widow Katie at Birch Grove that he rehearsed to me what was to be his famous 'family silver' speech. It included the words 'but women, my Lords, have never understood economics!' Katie and I were appalled; for one thing because it was not true, and for another everyone would know which woman he was thinking of. Regretfully, he agreed to delete it, but I was not certain until I attended that marvellous occasion. I sometimes regret my contribution to what was his last great appearance on the political stage.

I remember him with much affection, as well as admiration. If he was an actor, at least he was a supremely good one, and as a raconteur he was incomparable.

At one dinner at Petworth in 1967 Diana Cooper, Judy Montagu and John Wyndham were in such vociferous form that for once Macmillan could not get a word in edgeways; but he seized an unexpected lull to intone 'Did I ever tell you of the day I lost the Duke of Devonshire?' and he had his audience. The story was rather improbable, but it was hilariously funny, and we basked in the genius of The Master.

It is now almost Tory Party doctrine, and certainly was during the Thatcher reign, that all our national ills and the decline of true Toryism began during Macmillan's premiership. He is depicted as a cynical opportunist, with no real convictions, and essentially shallow. While recognising that at his best one had to get up very early in the morning to get the better of him, and that he had something of Arthur Balfour's ruthlessness, I believe that there was much more to him than that, and he is the only Prime Minister or former one who has been able to make me laugh. Sadly, his best stories – and especially one to the grave detriment of the reputation of Earl Mountbatten – are not contained in his Memoirs nor in his official biography.

But Hansard contains some gems. In his only Budget speech, in 1956, he held the House throughout, with his humour as much as with his content. At one point he quoted Dickens, and then sadly looked around the packed House, and asked 'But does anyone read Dickens nowadays?' and then, after a long mournful pause, 'Except the Russians?'

Perhaps his style palled, and aroused irritation rather than pleasures, but at least he had some, and it was real. The acting was the veneer rather than the substance, which was far more solid and deeply felt than his detractors would have us believe. But, as in the case of Pitt, they 'have not been under the wand of the magician'.

And what of the late lamented Duke of Devonshire, Macmillan's father-in-law?

'So far as I am aware, the ashes of the Duke of Devonshire are still travelling on the London and Northwestern Railway.' I did not believe it, but it did not greatly matter.

Whenever I returned to the House of Commons after a visit to Birch Grove I felt that I was among trivial pygmies. Perhaps this was unfair, but I had, once again, been under the wand of the magician, and had been bewitched. Others, it has to be said, were not, but nor were all Conservatives by Disraeli, although I would have been. There is something to be said for the exotic in Conservative politics.

2 'A Family Affair': Macmillan and the Art of Personal Diplomacy

Richard Aldous

It has been said that those who take up the sword shall perish by the sword. Certainly as far as Harold Macmillan is concerned, there is strong case for ascribing his political death in 1963 to the 'sword' of television, a medium which earlier he had exploited with alacrity. Macmillan was the first British Prime Minister to understand the significance of television and, although he feigned contempt for its intrusions, he used it to regain the propaganda initiative for the Conservative Party after the Suez Crisis. Presentation became a key component in the formulation of policy. Macmillan became 'Supermac', the urbane and witty Prime Minister at ease with himself and the affairs of state.

When Britain apparently moved into an era driven by the 'white heat of technology', Macmillan's Edwardian facade suddenly came to jar with the spirit of the times. Television programmes like *That Was The Week That Was* reflected and encouraged public dissatisfaction with an ageing Prime Minister, ridiculing him in ways unthinkable ten years earlier. ('Until then, there was respect', Edward Heath later grumbled.) Among the first to satirise Macmillan successfully was *Beyond the Fringe*. In the sketch *TV PM*, Peter Cook, aping the Prime Minister's *distrait* aristocratic style, told of recent travels 'round the world on your behalf and at your expense, visiting some of the chaps with whom I hope to be shaping your future'. Talks with President Kennedy had been 'of a very friendly nature and at one time we even exchanged photographs of our respective

9

families, and I was very touched, very touched indeed, to discover that here was another great world leader who regarded the business of government as being a family affair.' The tone was mocking but, like all good satire, it reflected a truth about its victim. Indeed, when Macmillan wrote in his memoirs about talks with de Gaulle at Birch Grove in November 1961, he recalled, just like the *TV PM*, that this had been a meeting of 'old buddies' and was 'a simple family affair'. The line between reality and art is often thin.[1]

Macmillan showed throughout his premiership a belief in the advantages of personal diplomacy at heads of government level. When he became Prime Minister in January 1957, he immediately resolved to meet President Eisenhower, with whom he had worked during the Second World War, in order to restore the Anglo-American relationship. Throughout Eisenhower's presidency, Macmillan blatantly attempted to manipulate the former Supreme Allied Commander's affection for Britain. This caused resentment among Britain's European allies and some considerable embarrassment to Eisenhower himself. Later in his premiership, Macmillan attempted a similar approach with President de Gaulle, another wartime contact, when thinking about Britain's entry into the European community.

Macmillan viewed the diplomatic process in unusually personal terms. Sometimes this was for the sake of publicity, as with his trip to Moscow in February 1959. But political expediency was not the only reason for his habitual dependence on personal relationships in executing foreign policy. Macmillan based most decisions on his own instincts, often ignoring the weight of bureaucratic and political opinion which advised to the contrary. For example, the success of diplomats on both sides in building a closer Anglo-German relationship[2] was cancelled out by Macmillan's own antagonism to Chancellor Adenauer, whom he thought 'a false and cantankerous old man'. Moreover, his understandably ambiguous feelings about Germans obscured his judgement on Franco-German relations. Convinced that for historical reasons a French President would never trust a German Chancellor, he aided the development of a close relationship between de Gaulle and Adenauer by treating them both rudely. The resulting Franco-German axis in Europe played a significant part in thwarting Britain's aims with regard to the EEC and the Western Alliance.[3]

Macmillan's time in office was punctuated by moments of personal drama. Indeed, when surveying the course of foreign affairs during that period, it is Macmillan's personal diplomacy which provides the defining moments of the premiership. When thinking in general terms about a national leader, there are often particular events or crises with which the name of that leader is associated. For example, we might think of Anthony Eden and Suez or John Kennedy and the Cuban Missile Crisis. When we apply the same test to Macmillan, it is talks which most readily come to mind. The meeting with Eisenhower in Bermuda, the Moscow visit, the summit at Paris, talks with Kennedy at Nassau and de Gaulle at Rambouillet. These are the key foreign policy moments in Macmillan's premiership.

Harold Macmillan's attraction to personal diplomacy was born to a significant extent of his own private circumstances. The impulses that drove him to pursue such an active personal role did not come simply from a cool analysis of Britain's world role. Macmillan's pursuit of a continuing global role for Britain was inextricably tied to his own hankering for recognition and prestige.

From his earliest years, Harold Macmillan had sought acceptance but never found it. His mother, Nellie, was a stern and manipulative woman who dominated young Harold's life in an intrusive and persecuting way. Her influence on him was tremendous. Nervous and sickly as a child, Harold was taught by Nellie to face adversity with courage, and had instilled the desire to win, at whatever cost, that made him such a tenacious political player. Yet, whatever his achievements, they were rarely sufficient to satisfy his mother's demands. This left Macmillan with a constant sense of failure. His frequently observed tendency to fawn and ingratiate himself owed much to this childhood reflex of always trying, without success, to please his mother. It was one of his greatest regrets that she died before he became

Prime Minister, the position she had always wanted for him.[4]

The sense of failure which Macmillan felt with his mother was intensified by the humiliations dealt to him by the Cavendish family. In March 1919, Macmillan's mother secured his appointment as ADC to the Governor-General of Canada, the Duke of Devonshire. Within months, he was head-over-heels in love with the Duke's third daughter, Lady Dorothy, and they married the following year. Dorothy was an 'outdoor' girl without intellectual pretensions. She had married Macmillan because he was the first man to show an interest, but quickly regretted her decision. She overcame her boredom by taking a lover, Conservative MP Bob Boothby, and took no trouble to hide her infidelity. The affair lasted more than thirty years and, aside from causing great personal anguish to the cuckolded Macmillan, humiliated him in the eyes of society. That humiliation was not eased by the appalling behaviour of her family. They treated him with unveiled contempt, despising his aristocratic pretensions if not his money. The Cavendish women thought him so dull that they drew lots to decide who would suffer sitting next to him at dinner. Weekends at Chatsworth were not easy for Macmillan.[5]

Denied loving acceptance by his mother, betrayed by his wife and ridiculed by her family, Macmillan was left to seek recognition in the most inappropriate place: the arena of politics. Here there was someone to emulate, a man who had achieved the public and international adulation that Macmillan himself so desperately wanted: Winston Churchill, 'the greatest Englishman of this, and perhaps of all, time'.[6]

From his first personal associations with Churchill in the 1930s, Macmillan was awestruck. Anthony Sampson has written perceptively that Macmillan was 'bowled over by the magnitude and romance of [Churchill]. Here was the complete man of action, the embodiment of history, with a vast vision of the world and destiny, with himself in the middle.' Throughout his career, Macmillan used Churchill as his role model, consciously affecting his mannerisms and style, advertising himself as Churchill's heir. Again, Macmillan's affections were not reciprocated. Churchill had no great love for him, always suspecting that the sentiment was bogus and self-serving. Macmillan's fawning irritated him and he often responded with abrupt rudeness. In short, Churchill and his entourage thought Macmillan was a bore and a creep, and certainly did not see him as a political heir.[7]

Given Macmillan's admiration of Churchill, it is not surprising that as Prime Minister he should attempt to conduct foreign policy in a 'Churchillian' style. Strategies like the 'Grand Design' of 1961 illustrate Macmillan's wish, like Churchill before him, to escape from the minutiae of government and see the 'bigger picture'. It was Churchill who provided the model for the way in which Macmillan conducted foreign policy negotiation using summitry and 'shuttle' diplomacy.

Macmillan had been fascinated with summitry and personal diplomacy since his earliest days in office. During the Second World War he had served as Minister Resident at the Allied Forces Headquarters in North Africa and gained first-hand experience of personal negotiations at the highest level. In January 1943, he attended the Casablanca conference with Churchill, which had an immediate and powerful effect on him. He breathlessly recorded in his diary that the conference had been 'like a meeting of the later period of the Roman empire', and christened Churchill and Roosevelt 'the Emperor of the East and the Emperor of the West'. The experience remained with Macmillan: the idea of bestriding the world stage as a latter-day Churchillian emperor appealed to his highly developed historical tastes.[8]

In a semantic sense, Churchill had invented summitry. On Valentine's Day 1950, he made a speech about the Cold War calling for a heads of government meeting and commenting: 'It is not easy to see how things could be worsened by a parley at the summit.'[9] This was the first time the word had been used in such a context. Back in power from 1951, Churchill's personal commitment to talks at the highest level almost precipitated the downfall of his own government. Churchill argued that because the West had a unitary military structure, NATO, it could now talk to the Russians from a position of strength. He proposed a series of summit meetings like the wartime conferences at Yalta and Potsdam, with wide agendas and the authority to cut deals. To start the process, he suggested flying off to Moscow for talks with Russian leaders. Ultimately, senior government ministers – including, ironically, Macmillan – could not believe that Churchill had the physical or mental resilience to conduct gruelling personal negotiations.[10] When Macmillan came to power in 1957, he picked up the Churchillian model for summitry, including proposals for a trip to Moscow, and took advantage of changed domestic and international circumstances to implement the policy.

Despite his advice to the Queen on taking office that a new government might not last 'more than six weeks', Macmillan's position as Prime Minister was strong. Conservative gossip in London's clubland said that the Suez débâcle would bring cataclysmic defeat at the next General Election and exile to opposition for the next twenty years. Those on both sides of the Suez divide recognised the electoral imperative of uniting behind Macmillan. This gave him tremendous power in setting his own agenda. When Cabinet colleagues attempted to constrain him, they were brushed aside. If they resigned in protest, as Salisbury and Thorneycroft did, their departure was dismissed as a local difficulty. In 1954, the threat of Cabinet resignations had taken Churchill's administration to the brink of destruction. In the wake of Suez, the Conservative Party could not afford such luxuries. MPs' self-preservation guaranteed Macmillan's position until the election. If Labour had won that election, he would almost certainly have been killed off as party leader.[11]

Macmillan's ability to control the political agenda was enhanced by his installation of a 'kitchen cabinet' at 10 Downing Street. This was a small group of advisers and officials whose first loyalty was to Macmillan. Principal among this group were 'Freddie' Bishop and Philip de Zulueta. They sacrificed high-flying careers to remain in Macmillan's private office and provided him with advice that was original and imaginative. It was men like Bishop and de Zulueta who were the 'change agents' essential to any process of redefinition. They gave Macmillan access to ideas that had not been dulled by slow passage through the bureaucratic machine. Their ascendancy in foreign affairs was accentuated by the weak political position of the Foreign Secretary, Selwyn Lloyd. He lacked a strong parliamentary or party base, and was beholden to Macmillan for his job. As the Prime Minister's creature, he was expected to do as he was told or else face dismissal. The initiative in setting the foreign policy agenda came not from King Charles Street but from 10 Downing Street.

Harold Macmillan's premiership was littered with personal discussions with international leaders on almost every important problem in Britain's foreign affairs. Probably the most notorious of these was his 1959 trip to see Khrushchev. It was, in the Prime Minister's own words, 'a startling and almost sensational event'.[12] When Macmillan stepped off his Comet IV on 21 February, he became the first British Prime Minister to visit Russia since the Second World War. Resplendent in a foot-high white fur hat, he cut quite a dash for waiting Soviet officials and the world's press. With the crisis atmosphere of the Berlin Ultimatum providing a suitable mood, Macmillan grandly announced that he had come 'to alleviate some of the cares that at present bring anxiety to the world'. This was, according to the everfaithful *Daily Mail,* an 'ice-breaking mission' for which 'Mankind will be in his debt.'[13]

Macmillan experienced tremendous highs and lows during his visit to the Soviet Union. At the outset, Khrushchev paid him every courtesy, hosting grand banquets at the Kremlin Great Palace and laying on a varied programme of entertainment which included sending them both careering down an ice-shute in a basket. First talks were courteous and accompanied by liberal quantities of Cuban cigars, vodka and caviar. The Russians did not change their position on matters of substance but Macmillan took comfort from their softening tones. The first few days, he recalled 'more than satisfied our expectations'.[14]

When the mood changed, it did so with sudden brutality. On 24 February, while Macmillan visited the Nuclear Research Institute at Dubna, Khrushchev made a provocative speech about Berlin, speaking of Eisenhower, de Gaulle and Adenauer in scathing terms. He offered an immediate Anglo-Soviet non-aggression pact, a seemingly clumsy attempt to separate Britain from its NATO allies. Discussions the following day were angry and fraught, with loose talk of a third world war. Voices were raised and tempers lost, not helped by the fact, Macmillan later sheepishly admitted, that 'we had all got rather drunk' before the meeting. The next day, 26 February, Khrushchev humiliated Macmillan with a public snub. He told the British that he would not be going to Kiev with them as planned. He had (diplomatic) toothache and needed to see a dentist. The British press was in no doubt about the significance of Khrushchev's change of plan. As the *Daily Herald* succinctly observed: 'Mr Macmillan's mission to Moscow is a complete failure'.[15]

With Macmillan ridiculed by the international press and a laughing stock in capitals around the world, the Prime Minister and his team acted quickly to retrieve the situation. In Kiev, Lloyd undertook a secret mission to see Kuznetsov, Soviet Deputy Foreign Minister. The Foreign Secretary amazed him by saying that Britain was prepared to recognise East Germany. The situation in Berlin had reached crisis point, admitted Lloyd, and Britain would not object 'if the Soviet Union wished to create a successor state [but] they must see that the state carried out the existing obligations' on Berlin. This was a sensational departure from the stated NATO position and its effect on the Russians was immediate. When the British party arrived in Leningrad, it was met unexpectedly by Gromyko and Mikoyan. They passed to Lloyd an advance copy of a Soviet note agreeing to foreign ministers' and heads of government talks about Berlin, effectively dropping the six-month deadline imposed by Khrushchev the previous November. Khrushchev returned to the role of genial host, telling everyone that his tooth had been cured 'by a British drill' (an amusing reference to Lloyd). With his dignity restored, Macmillan flew home on

3 March; it was, rhapsodised the *Daily Mail*, 'a return in triumph'.[16]

When, on 5 February, Macmillan announced his intention to visit Moscow, there had been a widespread belief that the Prime Minister was electioneering. *The Times*, voice of the Establishment, rebuked cynics and argued that Macmillan had proposed the visit in order 'to take a positive step in exploring the mind of the Soviet leaders in the course of direct meeting'. But it was the cartoonist Vicky who came closer to the truth. Drawn next to a graph showing plummeting Conservative support, the cartoon – Macmillan told American Secretary of State, John Foster Dulles: 'Why of course my journey's *really* necessary!' The reality was that Macmillan's proposal for a Moscow visit was driven almost entirely by domestic imperatives, notably to avert imminent defeat at the next general election.[17]

Macmillan had been obsessed by the forthcoming election from his first day in office. He understood that defeat at the polls would certainly require his stepping down as party leader. There were long odds on a Conservative victory: Labour had been consistently ahead in opinion polls since the Suez crisis, and no party in the twentieth century had won three elections in succession. Macmillan had until May 1960 at the latest to shorten those odds and deliver electoral victory. The new Prime Minister quickly came to believe that his election chances were inexorably linked to the issue of *détente*. The American Embassy in London reported back to Washington: 'This has pretty much become "no. 1" subject in terms of British political and public attention.' That conclusion was supported by opinion polls which by January 1958 suggested that 83 per cent of those questioned favoured an immediate summit meeting.[18]

Domestic opinion in favour of an early summit was symptomatic of general public concern over matters of war. The development of thermonuclear weapons with massive destructive capability initiated widespread debate about national and even global destruction. Leading strategists like Basil Liddell Hart had condemned British nuclear strategy

as a 'great bluff' and questions were asked about the reliability of American nuclear protection in an age of mutual
US–Soviet nuclear vulnerability. Public fears about imminent holocaust found powerful, organised expression in
February 1958 with the formation of an influential pressure
group: the Campaign for Nuclear Disarmament. CND
called for the scrapping of all British nuclear weapons, the
end of tests and rejection of foreign missile bases. With its
simple message of 'Ban the Bomb', CND touched a nerve in
public opinion and won considerable popular support.[19]

The rise of CND was potentially disastrous for Macmillan
and the Conservatives. Public opinion was demanding a
breakthrough in East–West relations to alleviate the threat of
nuclear holocaust. The Left had seized the initiative and was
streaking ahead in opinion polls. Macmillan had to find some
way to snatch it back. The Moscow visit was the outrageous
way in which he did so. As John Foster Dulles acutely observed to President Eisenhower in January 1959, Macmillan
proposed the Moscow trip because 'he faces an election, probably in the fall, and wants to be the hero who finds a way out
of the cold war dilemma'. As an electoral strategy, it was a brilliant response to domestic feeling. Polls taken immediately
after Macmillan's trip showed the Conservatives ahead for the
first time since the Suez crisis. When the Tories won an overwhelming victory at the general election in October 1959,
fought on a platform of 'Peace and Prosperity', only 8 per
cent of those questioned in polls said they were 'especially
concerned' about the H-bomb. It seemed that most people
agreed with the *Evening Standard* that Macmillan had made
'the world a more placid, less jittery place to live'.[20]

Domestic considerations were at the forefront of
Macmillan's mind when planning the Moscow visit. Other
foreign policy considerations, particularly relations with the
Western powers, counted for very little. For a man who took
so much pride in his relationships with the leading figures
of the Western Alliance, Macmillan paid scant regard to the
small courtesies that oil the wheels of friendship.

When Macmillan made his first direct approach to
President Eisenhower about the Moscow visit, his explana-

tion for the trip was insultingly transparent. He told the President that his real objective was to come to America for talks but 'in a curious way the best thing to do would be for me to get to Washington via Moscow'. This, he wrote, might stop the French and Germans misinterpreting the Washington visit 'as a sign of the intimate Anglo-American friendship of which they are so jealous'. 'It looks a little obvious,' commented a clearly unimpressed Eisenhower. He had already made clear to British Ambassador Harold Caccia his opinion that a trip to Moscow would be 'particularly dangerous' in the current crisis but reluctantly agreed that Macmillan 'can call there ... [But] he can't speak for us.' Secretly, Eisenhower hoped that the British would 'come back with their tails between their legs and then we are smart fellows'.[21]

Macmillan's treatment of Eisenhower was a little disingenuous but it was as nothing compared to the display of bad diplomatic manners shown to de Gaulle and Adenauer. Neither leader was consulted about the visit; both were informed of the impending visit just two days before the official announcement, in the House of Commons. The slight was felt very keenly, especially in Bonn, where all the talk was of British Appeasement, and had the effect of driving the Germans into the arms of the waiting French. De Gaulle, who was fastidious about diplomatic courtesies, recognised an insult when he saw one but took comfort from the fact that Macmillan's behaviour helped in his wooing of Adenauer.[22]

The initiative for the Moscow visit had come almost entirely from Macmillan. He not only railroaded his plans past reluctant Western Allies but also connived to invite himself to Moscow without informing the Cabinet. Only Lloyd and Rab Butler were consulted about the visit before the Americans were approached (although with Butler's weakness for indiscretion it is unlikely that colleagues did not have their suspicions). A year earlier, the Cabinet had rejected Macmillan's plan for a personal trip to Russia, believing that 'a proposal on these lines would be likely to provoke anxiety and suspicion among our allies and to be interpreted in this country as indicating a weakening in the attitude hitherto adopted by the government'. By 1959, the likelihood of Allied hostility to the plan had, if anything, intensified but the probable reaction in the country had changed. Macmillan decided that such an initiative was vital to his election plans and the Cabinet was not given a second opportunity to thwart him. In 1954, similar behaviour by Churchill almost brought about the collapse of the government. Now, Cabinet Ministers might grumble like Lloyd that summiteering was the 'occupational weakness of any incumbent of No. 10', but Macmillan was the best (and only) Prime Minister they had. With an election looming, they needed to trust him. On 8 October, Macmillan rewarded their faith with rich electoral dividends.[23]

If the Moscow visit had been a personal triumph for Macmillan, the Paris summit in May 1960 was a humiliating disaster. This was the nadir of his fortunes in personal diplomacy, which he later described as 'the most tragic moment of my life'. Prospects for a useful meeting had looked bleak from the first day of the summit. On 1 May, the Russians had shot down an American U-2 aeroplane flying in Soviet airspace. After issuing several transparently false statements about the plane, the Americans were forced to concede that the U-2 was on a spying mission. To Khrushchev's amazement and horror, President Eisenhower took full responsibility for the flight, which he called 'a distasteful but vital necessity'. Eisenhower's complicity severely undermined Khrushchev's own position, with Party hardliners arguing that he had been duped by Ike's expressions of goodwill at Camp David the previous summer. When Khrushchev arrived in Paris for the summit, he was accompanied by the 'Rocket Marshal', Malinovsky, whose task was to ensure that the Russian leader took a tough line with the Americans, particularly on the question of a public apology for the U-2 flight.[24]

On 15 May, at the first meeting between Eisenhower, Khrushchev, Macmillan and de Gaulle, the Russian leader launched a vitriolic attack on the American President. He withdrew his invitation to Eisenhower to visit Russia, and

vowed not to return to the summit table until a new
President was in office, unless the current incumbent would
apologise for his government's 'bandit policy'. When
Eisenhower tersely refused to do so, the meeting broke up
and stalemate ensued. All attempts to get the summit
meeting back on track failed and, on 19 May, Khrushchev
left Paris. This was the last time that the leaders of the four
wartime allies would meet together at the summit until
November 1990.[25]

Macmillan had worked for more than eighteen months
to achieve a summit. By May 1960, almost his entire foreign
strategy was dependent on the success of the summit policy.
Even before he became Prime Minister, Macmillan had
argued that it was 'external expenditure' which had
'broken our backs'. By 1960, the British economy, with its
crippling balance of payments deficit, was in no position to
withstand the financial pressures that went with global responsibilities. To address the problem, Macmillan initiated
early in his premiership a far-reaching review of Britain's
world role. It was headed by Sir Patrick Dean of the Foreign
Office who reported to a steering committee headed by
Cabinet Secretary, Sir Norman Brook. The final document,
Future Policy, 1960–1970, was circulated to the Cabinet in
February 1960. At 'the heart of the whole report', wrote
Dean to the Foreign Secretary, was 'the need to avoid an ab-
solute choice between North America on the one hand and
the continent of Europe on the other; that we should rather
aim to bind together one comprehensive Atlantic community.'[26] By putting Brook in charge, Macmillan had ensured
that the report matched his own thinking. Until 1960, it had
been generally assumed within policy-making circles that
Britain would have to make a choice between loyalty to
the Anglo-American 'special relationship' or the ever-
strengthening EEC. Using the rigged device of the Future
Policy committee, Macmillan signalled his rejection of that
notion and demanded that Britain belong to both camps,
acting as intermediary between them.

Summitry was the practical way in which Macmillan expected to fulfil that agenda. He set out to establish a system,

not unlike the nineteenth century Holy Alliance, whereby heads of government would meet at regular East–West and Western summits. Taking his lead from de Gaulle's famous memorandum of May 1958, Macmillan hoped to set up a ruling triumvirate of Britain, France and America for the Western Alliance. This would enable Britain to retain its influence on the world stage whilst shedding its expensive global responsibilities. As Lloyd commented to Macmillan, Britain had 'a number of albatrosses' around its neck but they could be 'disposed of without necessarily surrendering British interests'. Coming to the essence of British thinking, he continued: 'As we do so, we shall steadily grow stronger in influence. I do not believe size or physical military power alone will decide the future.' Throughout his premiership, Macmillan attempted to see the 'bigger picture' and responded to problems with grandiose strategies for change. The summit policy was an attempt to create a system that would allow Britain to use its worldwide prestige to retain influence whilst undergoing a process of retrenchment. Like de Gaulle in France, Macmillan expected to maintain the illusion of grandeur by replacing actual presence with influence.[27]

Macmillan had taken a very strong personal lead in setting up the summit policy and its rationale depended on his own ability to influence other leaders in face-to-face discussions. So it is particularly important that Macmillan performed so badly at Paris when dealing with the most important friendship of all, that with President Eisenhower. There is little doubt that Eisenhower had a certain affection for Harold Macmillan. The Prime Minister could be very amusing company and was always a sympathetic host. When Eisenhower visited London in August 1959, Macmillan took every trouble to make the visit a happy one. It was the small touches that he pulled off so well, such as placing himself at his wartime rank of Political Adviser for an official dinner, thus allowing Eisenhower to seat himself between Lords Alanbrooke and Alexander. When the President returned home, he wrote to Macmillan, with uncharacteristic emotion, that 'the unique and friendly character of this latest of our conferences ... was engendered ... by the close relationship between the two of us that seemingly grows stronger every time we meet'. The President enjoyed being fussed over by Macmillan and responded well to his sentimental reminiscences about the old days. Macmillan's error was to believe that genuine personal affection might win special favours at the conference table.[28]

Macmillan's misjudgement of Eisenhower at Paris was profound. When the President came to the summit, his credibility with American and world opinion was extremely low. The U-2 incident was a humiliation for him. By admitting to spying, the first President to do so publicly, he was accused of destroying America's moral authority in the battle against communism; involvement in the sordid world of espionage was not the behaviour expected from those fighting for the cause of 'righteousness'. Moreover, the U-2 incident exposed Eisenhower to the charge of incompetence. It gave the impression of a President who did not run his own administration, and a defence establishment that acted outside executive control. As Eisenhower's predecessor, Harry Truman, commented, America had been made to look 'ridiculous'. Ike had wanted to be remembered as a great peacemaker as well as warmaker. In the last eighteen months of his presidency he had hoped to make the world a safer place in which to live. Khrushchev's visit to Camp David, the summit in Paris and a historic presidential trip to Moscow were expected to provide a magnificent end to an outstanding life of public service. The U-2 incident destroyed those hopes and, according to his secretary, left Ike 'very depressed' and even considering resignation. He arrived in Paris shaken, angry and upset, only too aware that the meeting would 'not be a Sunday school picnic'. What he needed – and expected – was the support of those he called 'my old friends': Macmillan and de Gaulle.[29]

Macmillan had always made a great deal of his 'extraordinary relationship' with Eisenhower, even commenting implausibly that 'I was a sort of son to Ike'. If the Paris summit was an occasion when the President might have welcomed some filial affection, he was to be disappointed and angered by Macmillan's tepid loyalty. At the meeting of the four leaders, Khrushchev was rude and insulting towards Eisenhower. Macmillan himself recorded that Khrushchev had been 'vitriolic and offensive' and 'tried to pulverise Ike'. Eisenhower stayed calm and made a short, unapologetic statement. It was only on his return to the American embassy that he gave vent to his anger, shouting at staff that he was 'fed up!' with that 'son-of-a-bitch' Khrushchev. The President was still angry when Macmillan went to see him that evening, and, in the Prime Minister's understated words, 'relieved the tension by expressing in quite idiomatic language what he had thought about Mr Khrushchev and the Russians'. He was convinced that the summit was over and flatly refused to 'condemn the action which he had authorised'. Macmillan detected 'a certain uneasiness'about Eisenhower's manner that night which made his own lack of sensitivity all the more surprising. Eisenhower, having bared his soul to his old friend, now turned to him for support and consolation. What more could he have done, he asked the Prime Minister? Well, replied Macmillan, he could 'say he was sorry – or, preferably [make] a formal diplomatic apology.' It was not the answer Eisenhower had wanted.[30]

The President's view of Macmillan as a fair-weather friend was compounded by de Gaulle's attitude. When Khrushchev attacked Eisenhower, de Gaulle responded with a cutting speech. He rebuked the Russian leader for wasting everyone's time and condemned his hypocrisy in complaining about the U-2 when the previous day a sputnik 'overflew the sky of France eighteen times without my permission.' Spirited public defence was matched with private consolation. After the meeting, de Gaulle took hold of Eisenhower's arms and told him: 'Whatever happens, *we are with you.*' 'That de Gaulle is quite a guy,' Eisenhower later told an aide, adding that the General's words had 'really warmed [my] heart'. De Gaulle had been a thorn in the President's side for two years but now, when the American really needed his support, the French President had offered unhesitating loyalty. The strength of Eisenhower's gratitude was apparent in the letter he sent de Gaulle after the summit, in which he wrote: 'You and I have shared great experiences in war and peace, and from those experiences has come, for my part at least, a respect and admiration that I have for few men [. . .] Certainly the word "ally" has for me now an even deeper meaning than before.'[31]

Strengthened by de Gaulle, Eisenhower felt able to bring to bear on Macmillan his authority as head of the Western Alliance. After a meeting between the three leaders on the morning of 17 May, the American President startled Macmillan by inviting him to ride with him in his open top car. 'Ike's object was clear – ingenuously clear', the Prime Minister later recalled. 'If Khrushchev must break up the summit conference, there is no reason to let him break up the Anglo-American alliance'. Macmillan failed to recognise the obvious: Eisenhower sensed that the Prime Minister was trying to distance himself from the President and so avoid blame for the break-up of the conference. Making the PM travel with him was a public way of forcing Macmillan into solidarity. When, at a meeting later the same day, Macmillan suggested that they should seek out Khrushchev and 'beg him' to come to the summit table, Eisenhower finally lost all patience with the Prime Minister. He told Macmillan that his suggestion could only end in confusion and embarrassment', acidly reminding him that it was 'important to show unity at this juncture'. Rebuked in such a way, Macmillan conceded the point and sank into a deep depression.[32]

The summit was over and with it went Macmillan's attempts to establish a summit series. He would later comment melodramatically that 'the grand edifice which I had worked so long and so painfully to build seemed totally and finally destroyed.' Immediately after the conference, Macmillan confessed to Lloyd that it was 'difficult for the moment to see our way ahead' about summitry, particularly as he could no longer 'usefully talk to the Americans'. This was reinforced when the American National Security Council instructed that Allies be told that any attempt to initiate another summit 'would be interpreted as a sign of weakness'. The collapse of the summit policy was not just a problem for British policy: it had been a personal disaster for Macmillan. He had played his hand badly and left Paris in a much weaker position than when he arrived. He misjudged his 'friend' Eisenhower and his vacillation severely weakened Anglo-American relations. He had done so at a time when de Gaulle was determined to play the role of loyal and trusted ally. Macmillan's mistake had been to overestimate the strength of Britain's voice at the negotiating table. Philip de Zulueta, Macmillan's trusted private secretary, recalled that Paris 'represented a real watershed' for the Prime Minister because 'this was the moment he suddenly realised that Britain counted for nothing'. It is not surprising that Paris should have left Macmillan feeling 'really cast down and glum'. In a letter to the Queen, he commented dejectedly: 'We have fallen from the summit into the deep crevasse.'[33]

Macmillan's sense of having plummeted from the summit was compounded by the election in November 1960 of John F. Kennedy to the American presidency. Young, bright and debonair, the new President was both literally and metaphorically born of a different century to Macmillan. During the first months after Kennedy's election, the Prime Minister became increasingly gloomy about the prospects of forming a decent relationship with the new President and, according to advisers, started 'feeling his age'. Macmillan's own instincts were confirmed by de Zulueta, who told him in February 1961: 'With President Eisenhower the appeal to sentiment and comradeship was more effective than intellectual argument. Clearly this will not be the case with Mr Kennedy.' The Private Secretary's conclusion that 'cosy chats ... will not impress Mr Kennedy or help to get better relations with him' was a depressing one for the Prime Minister. Macmillan had always attached importance to personal friendships as a diplomatic weapon. In early 1961, it seemed that he must 'somehow to convince him [JFK] that I am worth consulting not as an old friend ... but as a man who, although of advancing years, has young and fresh thoughts.' He could not have anticipated that, in fact, it would be his demeanour as the 'old campaigner' which would provide the basis for closest relationship of his premiership.[34]

The two leaders met for the first time at Key West, Florida, and Washington in the spring of 1961. Macmillan was impressed with the President from the outset. He was 'courteous, quiet, quick, decisive – and tough', as well as having 'something very eighteenth century' about him which Macmillan found endearing. But Kennedy's classical charms could not hide the fact that he did not regard Macmillan as his equal and was not interested in starting a 'special' relationship. Kennedy was dismissive of Macmillan's offer to act as broker in the Cold War and was already making plans to meet Khrushchev at a superpower summit. Macmillan's worst fears about a post-Ike ending of privileged access came when Kennedy authorised the Bay of Pigs landing just weeks after his Washington visit. Macmillan was neither consulted nor even informed about the plan before it was put into action. The landings at Cuba showed Macmillan, if he had doubted it, that the President of the world's most powerful country was going to act as he damn well pleased, and did not need the sanction of a British Prime Minister to do so.[35]

The turning point in Macmillan's relationship with Kennedy came by courtesy of Khrushchev. Kennedy met the Russian leader at Vienna in June 1961 and was shocked by his strong-arm political tactics. By the President's own admission, Khrushchev 'just beat the hell out of me'. ('Politics is a merciless business', the Russian later commented about the meeting.) The journey to Britain from Vienna, commented Kennedy's Air Force aide, was 'like riding with the losing baseball team after the World Series'. Arriving in London, Kennedy was angry and in low spirits, made worse by chronic back pain. At their first full meeting, Macmillan, sensing that JFK was fed up, gave a nonchalant flick of the hand and said: 'Mr President, you have had a tiring day, don't let's have this ... Why not come up to my room and we will have a little chat?' Kennedy seemed relieved by the suggestion and the two men sat consuming whisky and sandwiches for a few hours. It was exactly this kind of elegant casualness that so endeared Macmillan to Kennedy. Arthur Schlesinger, presidential aide and later Kennedy's official biographer, later commented on the 'considerable temperamental rapport' that the two leaders discovered at that meeting:

> Kennedy, with his own fondness for the British political style, liked Macmillan's patrician approach to politics, his impatience with official ritual, his insouciance with professionals, his pose of nonchalance, even when most deeply committed. Macmillan, for his part, responded to Kennedy's courage, his ability to see events unfolding against the vast canvas of history, his contempt for cliché, his unfailing sense of the ridiculous. They found the same things funny and the same things serious [. . .] They soon discovered that they could match each other's transitions from gravity to mischief and communicate in shorthand. It was as if they had known each other for life.[36]

During the next two and a half years, the personal relationship between Macmillan and Kennedy blossomed into friendship – a friendship that was kept well oiled by the British ambassador in Washington, David Ormsby-Gore, whom the President trusted 'as I would my own Cabinet'. When JFK was assassinated in November 1963, Macmillan felt the death like 'a personal bereavement'. Over the years he wrote long letters to the President's widow, who apparently took great solace from them. She wrote back to Macmillan, emphasising 'how much Jack loved you' and the 'inspiration' he had given the President. 'People will say', she told the former Prime Minister, '"Do you remember those days – how perfect they were?" The days of you and Jack.' Leaving aside the sentimentality which quite naturally crept into their letters, the correspondence between Macmillan and Jacqueline Kennedy revealed the genuine personal affection which JFK and the Prime Minister had shared.[37]

Most historians agree that the warm, personal relationship between JFK and Macmillan/Ormsby-Gore translated into special influence for Britain. During the Cuban missile crisis, the British ambassador contributed to meetings of the National Security Council, making a critical suggestion about the 'quarantine line'. Throughout the crisis, JFK kept Macmillan in touch with events by telephone and requested his advice (but did not formally consult him). He even asked what Macmillan described as the $64,000 question: should he take out Cuba? When the crisis was over, Kennedy wrote to Macmillan expressing his thanks for 'your heartening support publicly expressed and our daily conversations [which] have been of inestimable value in these past days'. The missile crisis had been a superpower confrontation but Britain had at least had a direct line to the man with his finger on button, and in such circumstances, that gave some peace of mind.[38]

On a number of important issues, Kennedy remained accommodating to Macmillan's political needs and personal ambitions. The President tried to bolster Macmillan's position during the Profumo crisis by flying to Birch Grove for personal talks despite opposition from aides and American newspapers. On the peace question, an issue which the President had planned to address after the 1963 election, he responded to Macmillan's cajoling and agreed to a partial test ban treaty with the Soviets. 'So was realised at least one of the great purposes which I had set myself,' Macmillan later recorded. But the Prime Minister's personal influence on Kennedy was at its greatest during the Skybolt crisis. When the Americans finally admitted that Skybolt did not work, Macmillan insisted at a one-to-one meeting with the President at Nassau that Britain must have the opportunity to buy Polaris instead. Kennedy, belatedly aware that the issue was 'political dynamite' for Macmillan, scotched the objections of his own officials and gave the Prime Minister what he wanted. As Richard Neustadt has commented: 'It was a case of "king to king", and it infuriated the court.' It has been argued that the Polaris deal was a mistake because it reinforced Britain's dependence on the United States for its nuclear deterrent and alienated President de Gaulle. True as that might be, it does not detract from Macmillan's personal influence with Kennedy. The simple facts were that Macmillan went to Nassau and got exactly what he wanted thanks to Kennedy's personal intervention. Whether or not Macmillan used his influence wisely is entirely another question.[39]

Macmillan's relationship with JFK fulfilled at last his long-held expectations for personal diplomacy. Two decades earlier, he had watched with awe at Casablanca as Churchill sat in conference with Roosevelt, glorying in the Prime Minister's after-dinner tales of the 'Big Three'. With his sweeping vision and grand gestures, Churchill was the man above all others who Macmillan had wished to emulate. When he became Prime Minister in 1957, Macmillan had resolved to conduct diplomacy in a Churchillian fashion and this meant personal talks at the highest level. His drive towards the summit was undertaken with a determination bordering on the obsessive. It was a personal initiative taken in the face of Cabinet and Whitehall suspicions, exploiting their temporary weakness to brush aside objections.

Macmillan had not been afraid to use foreign policy to satisfy a domestic agenda. Certainly in 1959 he was more than happy to use a visit to Moscow to revive Conservative election hopes and victory at the polls seven months later seemed to vindicate the strategy. But Macmillan's use of personal diplomacy often had a serious detrimental effect on other British foreign policy issues. The Moscow visit, for example, alienated the French and Germans, opened the way for America to pursue superpower talks with the Russians without the British, and undermined the solidarity of the Western Alliance on Berlin. Similarly, Macmillan's personal deal with Kennedy on Polaris gave de Gaulle just the excuse he needed to justify vetoing the British application to join the EEC which delayed entry for another decade.

Macmillan's conduct of personal diplomacy sometimes appeared foolhardy but it was a genuine attempt to construct an overall strategy for Britain to use on the world stage. Like Churchill, Macmillan loved drawing up blueprints, such as the Grand Design, for a glorious British future. At the heart of all these plans was his own role as broker between America and a French-led EEC. Macmillan had strong faith in his own ability to influence other heads of government, but the simple truth is that, on most occasions, he was not very good at doing so. Adenauer clearly disliked him, a feeling which the Prime Minister reciprocated. Relations with de Gaulle were always courteous but, despite (or possibly due to) Macmillan's constant reminders about the 'old days', the French President always believed Macmillan to be a stooge of the Americans. Even Eisenhower, with whom Macmillan enjoyed a genuinely cordial relationship, refused to allow friendship to transcend American interests, as Macmillan discovered to his cost at the Paris summit.

But with JFK, Macmillan shared a genuine friendship which had dramatic consequences for Britain. Kennedy bestowed favours on his friend to help him out of political fixes. Macmillan responded with unfailing public support and sympathetic private hearings. Part of the reason for the relationship's success was that both leaders understood their place. After the Paris summit, Macmillan had apparently realised that 'Britain counted for nothing.' Therefore when he approached the new President, it was no longer as emperor to emperor (as with Churchill to Roosevelt, albeit a titular one) but more as nobleman to king. Offering his counsel and power in this way, Macmillan endeared himself to Kennedy, who enjoyed his friendship, trusted his loyalty, and respected his experience of international affairs.

Such influence as Macmillan enjoyed with Kennedy is glorious while it lasts but always remains ephemeral. Jacqueline Kennedy wrote to Macmillan after her husband's death that JFK had thought of him as 'almost an equal' – an epitaph which must have inspired equal measures of shame and pride in the former Prime Minister. But he would also have recognised that the special relationship which had existed between Britain and America between 1960 and 1963 died with the President in Dallas, if not at his own resignation. For personal relationships are unique to the personalities involved – a truism that Macmillan apparently failed to understand. Friendships can help to win spectacular advances but cannot serve as the focus for long-term strategy. With new leaders come new priorities and a different personal chemistry. The President's death revealed Macmillan's folly. In Washington, Britain went from being 'almost an equal' to almost a stranger. Only then did the full implication of rejection by Europe manifest itself, with Britain left to drift helplessly between two continents. Ten years later, Britain finally broke into the European Community. But it was another twenty years before a British Prime Minister had the influence in Washington that Harold Macmillan enjoyed with the young King at Camelot.

NOTES

1. *Sunday Times*, 29 August 1993; F. Muir and S. Brett, *The Penguin Book of Comedy Sketches* (London: Penguin 1992), p. 182; H. Macmillan, *Pointing the Way, 1959–61* (London: Macmillan 1972), p. 113 and photograph facing p. 408.
2. See Sabine Lee's essay in this volume.
3. A. Horne, *Macmillan Volume 2, 1957–1986* (London: Macmillan, 1989), p. 134; J. Lacouture, *De Gaulle: The Ruler, 1945–1970* (London: Collins Harvill, 1991), pp. 334–8.
4. P. Clarke, *A Question of Leadership: From Gladstone to Thatcher* (London: Penguin, 1992), pp. 211–12; R. Davenport-Hines, *The Macmillans* (London: Heinemann, 1990), p. 138; Horne, *Macmillan Volume 2*, pp. 4–5.
5. R. Rhodes James, *Bob Boothby: A Portrait* (London: Headline, 1991), pp. 112–13; Clarke, *Question of Leadership*, pp. 212–13; Davenport-Hines, *The Macmillans* (London: Heinemann, 1993), pp. 175–6.
6. H. Macmillan, *Riding the Storm, 1955–1959* (London: Macmillan, 1971), p. 189.
7. A. Sampson, *Macmillan: A Study in Ambiguity* (Harmondsworth: Pelican, 1967), pp. 77 and 89; Davenport-Hines, *The Macmillans*, p. 251.
8. H. Macmillan, *War Diaries: Politics and War in the Mediterranean, January 1943–May 1945* (London: Macmillan, 1984), p. 8.
9. J. Young (ed.), *The Foreign Policy of Churchill's Peacetime Administration, 1951–55* (Leicester: Leicester University Press, 1988), p. 55.
10. For a full examination of Churchill's summitry see: Young, *Churchill's Peacetime Administration*, pp. 55–80.
11. R. Blake, *The Conservative Party from Peel to Thatcher* (London: Fontana, 1985), pp. 278–81; Horne, *Macmillan Volume 2*, p. 8; Young, *Churchill's Peacetime Administration*, p. 68.
12. Macmillan, *Riding the Storm*, p. 559.
13. *Daily Mail*, 21 and 22 February 1959, p. 1; Macmillan, *Riding the Storm*, p. 594; for a full account of the Berlin Ultimatum see: J. Schick, *The Berlin Crisis, 1958–1962* (Philadelphia, 1971).
14. Macmillan, *Riding the Storm*, p. 604.
15. *Visit of the Prime Minister and Foreign Secretary to the Soviet Union, 21st February–3rd March 1959*: PRO (Kew), CAB133/293, pp. 29–33,

36–7; Horne, *Macmillan Volume 2*, p. 125; *Daily Herald*, 27 February 1959, p. 1.

16. Top Secret annex to *Visit of the Prime Minister to Soviet Union:* PRO (Kew), CAB133/293; Moscow tel. 403 to Foreign Office, 2 March, 1959: PRO (Kew) PREM11/2690; Sampson, *Macmillan*, p. 146; *Daily Mail*, 7 March 1959, p. 11.

17. *Daily Herald*, 6 February 1959, p. 1; *The Times*, 5 February 1959, p. 1; *Evening Standard*, 5 February 1959, p. 5.

18. Blake, *Conservative Party*, p. 281; State Department tel. 4544 from London, 3 February 1959: US National Archives (Washington DC) State Dept Decimal File, 1955–59, RG59/741.13; State Department tel. 4571 from London, 4 February 1959: US National Archives (Washington DC) State Dept Decimal File, 1955–59, RG59/741.13.

19. R. Taylor, *Against the Bomb: The British Peace Movement, 1958–65* (Oxford: Oxford University Press, 1988), pp. 26–7; I. Clark and N. Wheeler, *The British Origins of Nuclear Strategy, 1945–55* (Oxford: Oxford University Press, 1989), pp. 210–11.

20. Record of telephone conversation between Eisenhower and Dulles, 20 January 1959; Eisenhower Library (Abilene), Whitman File, DDE Diary Series 38 (Telephone Calls, January 1959); D. Butler and R. Rose, *The British General Election of 1959* (London, 1960), p. 71; *Evening Standard*, 1 September 1959, p. 4.

21. Foreign Office telegram 414 to Washington, 20 January 1959: PRO (Kew), PREM11/2775; Record of telephone conversation between Eisenhower and Dulles, 21 January 1959: Eisenhower Library (Abilene), Dulles Papers, Telephone Call Series 13 (White House Telephone Calls, January–April, 1959); Record of telephone conversation between Eisenhower and Dulles, 20 January 1959: Eisenhower Library (Abilene), Whitman File, DDE Diary Series 38 (Telephone Calls, January 1959).

22. CC(59) 4th conclusions, minute 1: PRO (Kew), CAB128/33; Lacouture, *De Gaulle: The Ruler* (London, 1991), pp. 334–8.

23. CC(59) 4th conclusions, minute 1, 3 February 1959: PRO (Kew) CAB128/33; CC(58), 8th conclusions, minute 4, 22 January 1958: PRO (Kew), CAB128/32; D. Thorpe, *Selwyn Lloyd* (London: Jonathan Cape, 1989), p. 297. Even senior and trusted figures like Lord Home were not consulted. Writing to him after the Soviets had agreed to the visit, Macmillan commented: 'I trust you feel that it is right to have taken this initiative.' PM to Commonwealth Secretary, 3 February 1959: PRO (Kew), FO371/143433.

24. Horne, *Macmillan Volume 2*, p. 231; for a comprehensive account of the U-2 incident see M. Beschloss, *Mayday: Eisenhower, Khrushchev and the U-2 Affair* (London: Harper & Row, 1986); Statement by the President, 11 May 1960: Eisenhower Library (Abilene), Whitman File, International Series 11, Paris Summit (1).

25. Conference of Heads of State and Government, Paris, 14–19 May 1960: PRO (Kew), FO371/1714.

26.   R. Holland, *Pursuit of Greatness: Britain and the World Role, 1900–1970* (London: Fontana, 1991), p. 279; Dean to Foreign Secretary, 15 March 1960: PRO (Kew), FO371/152133.

27.   'What I envisage is a series of meetings, each one leading on to the next ... Even if a summit meeting was not to make any progress at all I would feel that it could nevertheless serve a useful purpose provided it led to a further conference.' Macmillan to Robert Menzies, Commonwealth Relations Office tel. 1060 to Canberra, 10 November 1959: PRO (Kew), FO371/145499; Macmillan, *Pointing the Way*, pp. 102–3; Macmillan to Lloyd, 22 December 1959, Lloyd to Macmillan 31 December 1959: PRO (Kew) PREM11/2996; Lloyd to Macmillan, 13 December 1959: PRO (Kew), PREM11/2985; A. Grosser, *The Western Alliance: European-American Relations since 1945* (London: Macmillan, 1980), p. 187; M. Harrison, *The Reluctant Ally: France and Atlantic Security* (London: Johns Hopkins University Press, 1981), pp. 52–3.

28.   Eisenhower to Macmillan, 5 September 1959: Eisenhower Library (Abilene), Whitman File, International Series 23, Macmillan 1–12/59 (6); Jebb to Lloyd, 8 April 1960: PRO (Kew), FO371/153914.

29.   New York Times Summaries, May 1960: Eisenhower Library (Abilene), Minnich Series 16; Beschloss, *Mayday*, p. 249 and p. 273; Diary, 9 May 1960: Eisenhower Library (Abilene), Whitman File, Whitman Diary Series 11; 444th meeting of the NSC, 9 May 1960: Eisenhower Library (Abilene), Whitman File, NSC Series 12.

30.   Macmillan, *Pointing the Way*, p. 205 and p. 208; Memorandum of conference with the President, 16 May 1960: Eisenhower Library (Abilene), Whitman File, DDE Diary Series 50, Staff Notes; Beschloss, *Mayday*, p. 290.

31.   Record of meeting between the four leaders, 16 May 1960: PRO (Kew), FO 371/1714, *Paris, May 1960;* D. Eisenhower, *The White House Years: Waging Peace, 1956–61* (London, 1961), p. 556; Beschloss, *Mayday*, p. 290; Eisenhower to de Gaulle, 18 May 1960: Eisenhower Library (Abilene), Whitman File, International series 12.

32.   Macmillan, *Pointing the Way*, p. 208; Record of meeting between Macmillan, Eisenhower and de Gaulle, 17 May 1960: PRO (Kew), FO371/1714, *Paris, May 1960;* Horne, *Macmillan, Volume 2*, p. 231.

33.   Macmillan, *Pointing the Way*, p. 195; Macmillan to Lloyd, 24 May 1960: PRO (Kew), FO371/152128; 445th Meeting of the NSC, 24 May 1960: US National Archives (Washington DC), National Security Actions, 1952–60; Horne, *Macmillan, Volume 2*, pp. 113 and 233.

34.   Horne, *Macmillan, Volume 2*, pp. 281–2; de Zulueta to Macmillan, 24 February 1961: PRO (Kew), PREM11/3326.

35.   Sampson, *Macmillan*, p. 221; Horne, *Macmillan, Volume 2*, pp. 292–300; Macmillan, *Pointing the Way*, pp. 335–9 and 348–53.

36.   M. Beschloss, *Kennedy v. Khrushchev: The Crisis Years, 1960–63* (London: Faber & Faber, 1991), pp. 224–5; Macmillan, *Pointing the*

Way, pp. 356–9; Horne, *Macmillan, Volume 2,* pp. 303–5; Kennedy to Macmillan, 10 June 1961:PRO (Kew), PREM11/3328; CC(61), 30th conclusions, minute 6, 6 June 1961: PRO (Kew) CAB128/35; A. Schlesinger, *A Thousand Days: John F. Kennedy in the White House* (London: André Deutsch, 1965), pp. 339–41.

37.   Horne, *Macmillan, Volume 2,* pp. 368 and 575–9.
38.   Horne, *Macmillan, Volume 2,* pp. 368–70 and 378; D. Reynolds, *Britannia Overruled: British Policy and World Power in the 20th Century* (London: Longman, 1991), p. 214.
39.   Horne, *Macmillan, Volume 2,* pp. 523 and 439; Schlesinger, *A Thousand Days,* pp. 736–9; Reynolds, *Britannia Overruled,* pp. 214–15.

3 Macmillan and the Middle East

Nigel Ashton

One of the great ironies of the Suez Crisis is that it resulted in the replacement of one Prime Minister, Anthony Eden, deemed to have taken too radical an approach in defence of British interests in the Middle East, by another, Harold Macmillan, whose views on the region were, if anything, even more radical. Macmillan was not only the foremost of the Cabinet hawks over Suez, and the first to propose the involvement of the Israelis in military action against Egypt, he was also responsible for the effective misrepresentation to Eden of the views of the US administration on the use of military force in cables sent during his visit to America in September 1956. Finally, and confusingly, it was the breaking of Macmillan's nerve during the Suez landings which more than any other single factor seems to have dictated the decision to halt operations on the morning of 6 November 1956.

Macmillan's apparent tergiversations led to the famous stricture of Harold Wilson that he was 'first in, first out' over Suez, and have led David Carlton to comment that with Macmillan, 'we may be dealing with nothing more than the cynical machinations of an opportunist intent on creating conditions in which he might have a chance to seize the premiership.'[1]

Whilst such machinations may well have played a part in the way in which Macmillan outmanoeuvred Butler in the struggle for the leadership of the Conservative Party following Eden's physical breakdown in mid-November, they do not satisfactorily explain his radical stance on Suez, which needs to be set in the broader context of his thinking on the Middle East both before and after the crisis. The focus here, therefore, will be not only on Macmillan's conduct of policy towards the region as Prime Minister, but also as Foreign Secretary during 1955, and as Chancellor of the Exchequer during the Suez Crisis itself. At the heart of the discussion will be the tension between Macmillan's desire to pursue a strategy designed to preserve particular British interests in the Middle East, and the more general interest in building and maintaining the Anglo-American alliance.

POST-WAR BRITISH STRATEGY IN THE MIDDLE EAST

The Eden government was of course in no sense novel in viewing the Middle East as an area on which depended the very national survival of the United Kingdom. The burgeoning importance of oil supplies drawn from the Gulf in the immediate post-war years, together with the significance of the region in the developing Cold War with the Soviet Union, had led Labour Foreign Secretary Ernest Bevin to tell his Cabinet colleagues in August 1949 that 'in peace and in war, the Middle East is an area of cardinal importance to the UK, second only to the UK itself',[2] Whilst there were of course differences in tactics between the post-war Labour governments and their Conservative successors, there was no disagreement on the central tenet of the strategic significance of the Middle East to Britain. Anthony Eden himself described it as 'of the greatest importance for the United Kingdom. We depended on it for our life.'[3]

Harold Macmillan was thus not exceptional amongst post-war British statesmen in the opinions he expressed on the region. Whilst in opposition, Macmillan's thoughts on Soviet aims in the Korean war, for instance, showed the strategic priority he attached to the Middle East. The attack in Korea, he believed, could be a feint, to pin the Americans down there, whilst the Russians started 'a drive in the Middle East, where the prize is really great – the greatest source of oil supply in the Old World.'[4]

Although not directly involved in foreign policy formation in the Churchill government of the early 1950s, Macmillan had also taken a tough line in Cabinet on withdrawal from the Suez Canal Zone base in Egypt leading to frequent clashes of opinion with Eden.[5] His fears about reducing the British military presence in the area were founded on the belief that Britain could not risk losing access to oil supplies vital to national survival.

MACMILLAN AS FOREIGN SECRETARY

It is well established that Macmillan had coveted the post of Foreign Secretary throughout his political career. His appointment to the office by Eden following the Conservative election victory of May 1955 gave him an opportunity to put into practice amongst other things some of his own ideas for British strategy in the Middle East. His principal inheritance in this respect was British membership of the Baghdad Pact, a regional defence organisation linking Iraq to Turkey.

The Pact was regarded by both Macmillan and Eden, who had negotiated Britain's entry as Foreign Secretary, as the new cornerstone of the British position in the region. It secured existing British defence rights in Iraq, and seemed to present the possibility of some new regionwide alliance, linking any further Arab states prepared to join to Britain, and securing her strategic interests in the area. The big problem with the pact was the opposition of the Egyptian leader, Gamal Abdel Nasser, to what he saw as a British and American inspired device promoting Iraqi leadership of the Arab world.

Because of American concerns that Egyptian opposition to the Pact might destabilise the whole region and provide the USSR with opportunities to intervene, Eden had been forced to accept the US suggestion of a moratorium on further Arab membership of the Pact during the summer of 1955, whilst the US and UK worked to diminish Nasser's hostility.[6] A principal plank of Macmillan's agenda as Foreign Secretary seems to have been to break this moratorium, and to set to work on building up the membership of the Pact. The most promising candidate as the next Arab state to join

Iraq in the Pact appeared to be Jordan, where Britain had existing political and defence interests secured by treaty.

The tactics Macmillan used to achieve his goal prefigure those which he was to employ in misrepresenting the American attitude to Eden during the Suez Crisis. Whilst it is important to say at the outset that in neither case did Macmillan force Eden into a policy he was not already inclined towards himself, he played a significant role in gingering the Prime Minister to act. In both cases, Macmillan seems to have presented an opinion of his own as that of his American interlocutor.

So, with regard to the question of securing Jordanian entry into the Baghdad Pact, Macmillan reported to Eden that, at a meeting in Geneva during the latter part of October 1955, the US Secretary of State had made the following comments:

> Mr Dulles asked me whether we could not bring pressure on Jordan to join the Baghdad Pact. He thought it would be a fine thing if they did. He regarded Jordan as our affair. He added that he thought we might consider trying to get Jordan to make a unilateral settlement of frontiers with Israel. If this could be done, leaving out Egypt altogether, it would be a great advantage.[7]

There is no reference in any of the American records of the conversations between Macmillan and Dulles during this period of the Secretary advocating pressure on Jordan to join the Baghdad Pact. This indeed seems rather incongruous in view of Dulles' previous advocacy of a moratorium on Pact membership, and his later statement that 'he rather wondered whether it was wise to bring ... [the Jordanians] in.'[8] The only US record of Jordanian accession to the Baghdad Pact being discussed by Macmillan and Dulles shows Macmillan advocating the move, with no recorded response from Dulles:

> Mr. Macmillan went on to say that he thought it might be good idea to try and push Jordan in the direction of its Hashemite cousins, Iraq. It might be that Jordan could be

induced to move toward a settlement with Israel if it had the backing of Iraq.[9]

Macmillan's words in the American version are put into Dulles' mouth in the telegram sent back by Macmillan to Eden. This falls into the pattern of Macmillan's attempts to promote the idea of Jordanian membership of the Pact in the face of a measure of reluctance on the part of Eden, who was 'beginning to wonder whether it was wise to press Jordan hard to join the Pact'. Macmillan was not above using a distorted version of the US attitude on this issue to keep the pressure on Eden.[10]

The more famous instance of such a distortion by Macmillan comes during the Suez Crisis itself when Sir Roger Makins, then British Ambassador in Washington, reported that Macmillan met Eisenhower for more than half an hour during a private visit to the US with nothing said at all on Suez. However, Macmillan cabled Eden that 'Ike is really determined, somehow or other, to bring Nasser down.'[11] Although Makins himself has charitably labelled this a failure in communications, in the light of Macmillan's behaviour as Foreign Secretary, we may have the beginnings of a pattern of distortion of conversations with the Americans, at important junctures, in communications from Macmillan to Eden, to assist in the promotion of policies favoured by Macmillan.

In the event, the attempt to get Jordan into the Baghdad Pact was to end in failure. After the collapse of the mission of Chief of the Imperial General Staff, General Templer, in the face of widespread rioting in the country during December 1955, Eisenhower confided to his diary: 'We tried to make the British see the danger of ... pressuring Jordan to join the Northern Tier Pact. They went blindly ahead and only recently have been suffering one of the most severe diplomatic defeats Britain has taken in many years.'[12] This was a defeat for which Macmillan must bear a large measure of responsibility.

Whilst the situation was still unfolding in Jordan, Eden moved Macmillan from the Foreign Office to the Treasury.

Most commentators, and indeed Macmillan himself, seem to have taken this as an expression of the fact that Eden did not believe he could exercise as much control over foreign policy as he wished with Macmillan at the Foreign Office. There certainly seems to be some substance to this claim in view of his approach to the question of Jordanian accession to the Baghdad Pact.

MACMILLAN AND SUEZ

There is, of course, as indicated at the outset, something of a central paradox to be explained over Macmillan's behaviour during the Suez Crisis. It has already been established that Macmillan held strong views about the strategic importance of the Middle East to Britain. Moreover, as Foreign Secretary, he was willing to push forward his preferred strategy of enlarging and building on the Baghdad Pact, irrespective of the opposition of Nasser, the misgivings of the US administration, and the vacillations of Prime Minister Eden.

At the beginning of the Suez Crisis, in the fortnight immediately following Nasser's announcement of the nationalisation of the Suez Canal on 26 July 1956, Macmillan took if anything the most hawkish stance of any member of the Cabinet barring Eden as to the response Britain must make. Yet, in its concluding hours, it was his insistence that Britain would be broken financially if she fought on in the face of American opposition that more than any other single factor changed the mind of the Cabinet. How is Macmillan's behaviour to be explained, and what light does it shed forward on his conduct of policy toward the region on becoming Prime Minister?

Macmillan set out his stall on the crisis in discussions with Eisenhower's special representative, Robert Murphy, over dinner on 30 July. He warned Murphy that if Britain had to go down she would go down fighting. On the possibility of Soviet intervention in any British military operations against Nasser, he commented 'if we should be destroyed by Russian bombs now, that would be better than to be reduced to impotence by the disintegration of our entire position abroad.' Britain was ready not only to use force, according to Macmillan, but to despatch it immediately.[13] Macmillan confided to his diary that he had done his best to frighten Murphy so that he would report British determination to use force to Eisenhower and Dulles.[14] However, the substance of his comments on the necessity of using force to secure British interests and to humiliate or depose Nasser summed up his position throughout the crisis.

Macmillan followed up his initiative with Murphy on 3 August by raising the question of coordinating action against Nasser with the Israelis in the Egypt Committee, the special Cabinet cabal established by Eden to manage the crisis. His initiative took the form of a memorandum sent to Eden in which he proposed that with regard to military action against Egypt, 'the simplest course would be to use the immense threat to Egypt that results from the position of Israel on her flank ...' Eden was reportedly 'very shocked' by the suggestion.[15] However, Macmillan persisted in discussing the possibility and, at a meeting he chaired at 11 Downing Street the following day, involving amongst others Lord Salisbury and the British Ambassador to France, Gladwyn Jebb, the question of Israeli participation was again raised.[16]

On 7 August, Macmillan proposed a new plan for military action against Nasser to the Egypt Committee. This involved a much more wide-ranging operation than the original intention merely to occupy the Canal Zone. Its professed goal was to bring about the downfall of Nasser. Although Eden was apparently somewhat piqued by Macmillan's discussion of his initiative with Churchill, the Chancellor's initiative did result in a reconsideration of existing plans for military action.[17]

Macmillan seems to have remained convinced throughout the ensuing weeks of the crisis that military action against Nasser was both the inevitable and desirable way of resolving the Canal dispute. Certainly, his cynicism on the matter of negotiations with Nasser was to provoke an outburst from Walter Monckton, the doveish Minister of

Defence, towards the end of August on the moral implications of such an attack.[18]

The crisis also afforded several glimpses of what might be termed Macmillan's 'grand design' for the region. At the meeting he held with Salisbury and Jebb on 3 August, in addition to discussing the possibilities of Israeli participation in a conflict with Egypt, Macmillan aired broader ideas about a refashioning of the political order in the Middle East along lines favourable to Britain. Schemes considered included, not surprisingly, the expansion of the Baghdad Pact, and the creation of the so-called Fertile Crescent. The latter involved the bringing together of Syria, Jordan and Iraq in an Iraqi dominated confederation, and would further the strategy of building Britain's position on the back of Iraqi leadership of the Arab world.

Later in August, Macmillan sent Eden a memorandum again showing his penchant for extravagant thinking as regards the future of the area. Britain, Macmillan asserted, should not be like Louis XVIII creeping back to France, but like Napoleon bursting onto the plains of Italy. She should not stop at the mere occupation of Egypt, but should summon a conference of all the states of the region and draw up a plan for the future of the whole of the Middle East. Boundaries should be settled, with the disappearance of unviable creations such as Jordan. Macmillan evidently envisaged a settlement like that of 1921, in which a British Cabinet Minister determined the frontiers of the Levant.[19]

Macmillan's most significant contribution to the build-up to military intervention during September was his report to Eden of conversations with Eisenhower and Dulles discussed above during a private visit to the US. Although some commentators, including Macmillan's official biographer, have been inclined to treat his misrepresentation charitably,[20] it seems clear that Macmillan's behaviour followed a pattern of repackaging of American opinions to suit his own purposes which he had already established whilst at the Foreign Office.

Macmillan's diaries of the crisis end in early October at around the point when collusion with the French and Israelis may have been started to be considered.[21] However, in view of his continuous enthusiasm for military action against Nasser, and his earlier suggestion that Israelis might be involved in some way, it is doubtful whether he needed much persuading of the advantages of the scheme. Certainly, at no point before the start of military operations in early November did he display any reluctance to follow the attack on Egypt through. It was in the final hours of the crisis, when landings by British and French forces on the Canal had already begun, that Macmillan's nerve was to break spectacularly.

The reason Macmillan presented for his change of mind was that the British military action had precipitated a run on sterling which, if not checked, could result in the collapse of the sterling area and unthinkable economic damage to the nation. Macmillan apparently told his Cabinet colleagues that the foreign currency reserves had fallen by $280 million in the first week of November, a figure that represented around one-eighth of the total reserve.[22] The drain could only be checked by drawing down resources from the International Monetary Fund or securing a loan from the US. Either way, Britain could only act with American assistance. The open hostility of the US administration to the British action meant that such help would not be forthcoming whilst military operations continued.

Although the US administration's policy was founded on Eisenhower's outrage at British actions, it was Assistant Secretary of State Hoover and Treasury Secretary Humphrey who dealt with Macmillan during Dulles' absence in hospital. Both had a reputation for suspicion of Britain as an imperialist power. It was evidently a conversation with Humphrey early in the morning of 6 November which brought home to Macmillan the depth of American hostility. In it he was told flatly that assistance would be out of the question unless a ceasefire had been arranged by midnight that night.[23] The crucial factor in bringing about

Macmillan's change of heart, therefore, seems to have been the belief that Britain could not continue to act in the face of such open American opposition.

This fact, taken together with Macmillan's attempts to rebuild the Anglo-American relationship once he had assumed the premiership after Eden's resignation, has been presented by most commentators on Suez to show that from now on, under Macmillan, Britain would no longer endeavour to pursue an independent strategy in the Middle East. Scott Lucas, for instance, asserts that after Suez, 'Britain paid the price of permanent subservience to American policy.'[24] It is certainly true that after Suez Anglo-American channels of communication and consultation were to be improved substantially. However, as will be seen, the revived Anglo-American relationship was always to be used as a means towards established British ends by Macmillan, rather than as an end in itself. Although Macmillan would never again push Anglo-American differences over the Middle East to the point of open rupture, he would equally not trim British strategy in the region to suit the US administration. The Anglo-American relationship in the Middle East, as no doubt elsewhere, involved in Macmillan's mind trying to turn American power and resources towards the achievement of British ends.

It must be admitted, however, that the Suez defeat administered a profound shock to morale in Britain. Not only this, but it left the Prime Minister Anthony Eden a physically broken man. The weeks from the decision to halt operations on 6 November until Macmillan's succession to the premiership on 9 January 1957 witnessed Macmillan using his skills of political manipulation to the utmost. The man who more than anyone else had precipitated the halt to military action managed to cast his principal rival for the premiership, 'Rab' Butler, in the light of the bolter. This success, however, should be seen more as an example of political opportunism, than as the culmination of any deeper-seated plan, such as that envisaged by David Carlton, to take over the premiership by setting out a radical stall on the Middle East. Such explanations simply invest Macmillan

with far too much foresight as to the likely course of events
during 1956.[25]

PRIME MINISTER MACMILLAN AND THE MIDDLE
EAST, 1957–59

Once Macmillan had gained the prize of the premiership,
he was in a far better position to pursue his agenda in the
Middle East. As Keith Kyle has noted, 'If there had been one
person more set on destroying Nasser than Eden it had been
Macmillan.'[26] The central plank of Macmillan's policy, therefore, was to be an attempt to enlist American support in operations to extirpate Nasser's influence from the region.
Macmillan like Eden had identified Nasser as the most direct
threat to British interests in the Middle East as far back as
March 1956. Suez and the humiliating climbdown which
followed served only to heighten the new Prime Minister's
hostility towards the Egyptian leader. At the Bermuda
Conference of March 1957, President Eisenhower noted
that: 'Foster and I at first found it difficult to talk construc-
tively with our British colleagues about Suez because of the
blinding bitterness they felt toward Nasser.' They were, according to the President, 'obsessed with the possibilities of
getting rid of Nasser'.[27]
    Although much was done at Bermuda to restore the at-
mosphere of conviviality between the leaders of the two
countries, little was done to bring them closer together over
strategy in the Middle East. Both Eisenhower and Dulles
were concerned that the Soviet Union would take the opportunity to profit from the power 'vacuum' created in the
region by the Anglo-French defeat. During the course of
November and December 1956, the US administration had
come under great pressure from the regional members of
the Baghdad Pact, Iran, Iraq, Turkey and Pakistan, formally
to join the organisation to fill this vacuum.[28] Britain too had
pressed her appeals in this respect once again.[29]
    As an expedient to avoid joining the pact which was com-
promised in his eyes as an instrument of British policy,

Dulles had hit upon the Eisenhower Doctrine, an anti-communist declaration made by the President in January 1957 which offered economic and military assistance to states in the Middle East requesting aid against 'armed aggression from any country controlled by international communism'.[30] The other element of American policy was to be the intensification of efforts, begun as early as March 1956, to promote the role of King Saud as leader of the Arab world in rivalry to Nasser.[31]. This policy was unwelcome to Macmillan, not only because it was to be pursued in rivalry to his own preferred approach of continuing to promote the influence of Iraq, but also because it created complications for Britain in the Arabian Peninsula, where various of her protectorates had territorial disputes with Saudi Arabia.

On Nasser too, differences remained largely unresolved. Although both sides could agree that in the short term Nasser's influence in the region was pernicious, a vital element of pragmatism remained in the US approach to the Egyptian leader which was lacking in Macmillan's view at this stage.[32] Still, on a more positive note, it was at least agreed at Eisenhower's initiative to set up a Joint Planning Staff in an effort to bridge the gap between the policies of the two countries in the Middle East.[33] Also, the President announced the US's willingness to join the military committee of the Baghdad Pact. However, as Foreign Secretary Selwyn Lloyd had earlier commented, this, from the British point of view, was 'very much a second best and no substitute for full accession to the pact'.[34]

Thus, although the Bermuda Conference took much of the rancour out of Anglo-American relations over the Middle East, significant differences in strategy between Macmillan's government and the US administration remained. Macmillan sought to continue to build up the role of Iraq and the Baghdad Pact in the region, whereas Eisenhower's preference was to promote the role of King Saud of Saudi Arabia. Macmillan remained preoccupied with the threat to British oil interests in the Middle East presented by the revolutionary Arab nationalism of Nasser, whereas Eisenhower was more concerned with the threat of 'international communism'. In comparison to this threat Nasser, as Eisenhower would later remark, was 'so small a figure, and of so little power, that he is a puppet, even though he probably doesn't think so.'[35] He would be dealt with more pragmatically, on the basis of assessments of his closeness to the Soviet Union at any particular time. What these differences in strategy and perceptions of threat would produce in the region was a patchwork of conflict and cooperation between the two countries bearing many similarities to relations in the years before the Suez Crisis. In this respect it seems justified to speak of a large measure of continuity in Anglo-American relations in the Middle East before and after the Suez Crisis.

The first opportunity for Macmillan to enlist US support in the struggle with Nasser seemed to be provided by the crisis which broke out in Syria in August 1957. The expulsion of three American diplomats for spying activities, together with the appointment of a supposed communist sympathiser to head the army and the signature of a trade and technical agreement with Moscow, led US Secretary of State Dulles for one to believe that a Soviet-backed coup was imminent in Syria. In the first instance, Dulles believed that Nasser was cooperating with the Soviets in organising the coup. The coincidence of the two threats enabled Macmillan to play on Dulles' fears of communism to establish a new framework for the exchange of diplomatic, military and intelligence material on Syria.

The so-called 'Syria Working Group' was a flexible mechanism for Anglo-American consultation, meeting on the request of one or other party in response to the rapid changes in the situation in Syria.[36] It seemed to mark the first step along the course Macmillan had charted of enlisting American assistance to achieve British goals in the Middle East. Certainly, he himself referred to it as the beginnings of a 'great new venture' between the two countries.[37]

During the Syrian crisis, Macmillan's 'grand design' for the Middle East seems to have surfaced once again. Certainly, discussions of the problems of Syria found him advocating broad and extravagant solutions. Reflecting in

Cabinet on the fact that pipelines carrying Iraqi and Saudi Arabian oil passed through Syria, he argued that:

> It was ... important that no action should be taken which might provoke Syria to cut these pipelines unless it formed part of a considered plan, which the United States Government were prepared to carry through, for restoring the whole position in the Middle East in favour of the Western Powers. It should not be overlooked that action which led the Syrians to interfere with the pipelines might also cause the Egyptian Government to restrict the passage of oil through the Suez Canal ...[38]

Macmillan at this stage seems to have envisaged the possibility of a broader Middle Eastern war in which the US, as a result of the combined planning for operations against Syria undertaken by the Working Group, might be drawn into backing Iraq alongside Britain against Egypt and Syria. In a 'Top Secret' memorandum sent to the Minister of Defence, Duncan Sandys, marked 'personal' and 'not to be shown to the Chiefs of Staff', he put the question:

> In the event of Iraq finding itself at war with Syria and Egypt attacking Iraq, if Iraq calls upon us under the Treaty to come to her aid, what military measures should we be able to take and what military consequences might be entailed? ... It would be assumed for this purpose that the United States would also be bringing help to Iraq and would be taking military measures against Egypt.[39]

In the event, although the Syria Working Group continued to function, and indeed formed the model for a broader range of such groups set up after the Sputnik launch and Macmillan's October 1957 visit to Washington, British and American policy in the Middle East began to move apart again once it was clear that Nasser was not cooperating with the Soviets over Syria. Indeed, by the end of the year, following a secret approach from Nasser, Assistant Secretary of State William Rountree was advising the US Ambassador in Cairo to tell the Egyptian leader that the administration 'would welcome action designed [to] impede

[the] Communist threat [to the] security of Syria and [the] entire ME [Middle East].' Moreover, the administration would 'wish [to] avoid impeding any Egyptian efforts to bring about change' in the region.[40] This attitude of 'getting along with Nasser' as Dulles termed it, before and after the creation of the United Arab Republic of Egypt and Syria in February 1958, helps to explain the considerable exasperation of British officials with US policy in the Middle East during the early months of 1958.[41]

A further opportunity for Macmillan to enlist US support in the struggle with Nasser, however, seemed to be provided by the civil disorder which broke out in Lebanon in May 1958. Since the Lebanese President, Camille Chamoun, had been the only leader in the region enthusiastically to embrace the anti-communist Eisenhower Doctrine promulgated at the beginning of 1957, US Cold War credibility was heavily engaged in the survival of his regime. The threat to his position provided by the outbreak of unrest, and the belief on the US part that this must be communist-inspired, led to a renewal of military and diplomatic cooperation with Britain. Contingency planning for joint Anglo-American military operations in the Levant was restarted in the middle of May. The result was a plan for intervention in the event of a serious breakdown in order in Lebanon code-named 'Blue Bat'.[42]

Macmillan again sought to capitalise on the situation in pursuit of his broader goals. Rumours abounded in Washington that the British were behind the Lebanese government's decision to take the issue of interference by Nasser's United Arab Republic in its internal affairs to the United Nations Security Council. This was believed to be part of an attempt to bring the conflict with Nasser to a head, and, in the words of the US United Nations representative, Henry Cabot Lodge, 'wipe the slate clean re Suez'.[43] This opinion was repeated by UN Secretary General Dag Hammarskjöld.[44] Dulles himself conceded that the British were 'trying to push us in more rapidly than we want to go'.[45]

In the event, it was the bolt from the blue occasioned by the Iraqi revolution of 14 July which brought Macmillan's 'grand design' in the region into the open once more. The coup which overthrew the Anglophile Hashemite regime in Baghdad on the morning of 14 July seemed initially to Macmillan to be the work of Nasser, and to provide the opportunity to draw the US into wide-ranging operations in the region alongside Britain of the kind which he had envisaged a year earlier over Syria. On the evening of 14 July, in a telephone conversation in which Eisenhower advised him of the US decision to intervene in Lebanon in response to a request from President Chamoun, Macmillan told the President: 'The point is this. If you do this thing in the Lebanon, it is really only part of a much larger operation, because we shall be driven to take the thing as a whole. I want to feel that we both regard it as a whole. It looks like a showdown.'

Eisenhower's response to Macmillan was decidedly cool. 'So far as we are concerned we cannot undertake anything beyond Lebanon. The situation elsewhere is going to be much more complicated,' he replied.[46] Having agreed to the shelving of 'Blue Bat', the contingency plan for joint intervention in the Lebanon, and acquiesced in the US acting unilaterally, Macmillan spent the next two days trying to create the circumstances in which King Hussein of Jordan would request British troops to enter his country to give the appearance that Britain was acting alongside America. At the same time, he endeavoured to persuade Eisenhower and Dulles of the necessity of British intervention. Both, however, were suspicious of the move. Eisenhower noted that 'the UK wants to get us to commit ourselves now to clearing up the whole mid-East situation, and this gives ... [me] a good deal of concern.[47]

In the event, in what has all the hallmarks of a put-up job, British intelligence conveniently discovered that a coup against King Hussein was due to take place on 17 July, leading him to request the support of British forces, and enabling Macmillan to get troops into the region. His statements to the House of Commons on the matter disclaiming any prior knowledge of the King's request and describing the decision to intervene as one of the hardest he had ever taken appear disingenuous in the extreme.[48] In fact, in a meeting with Duncan Sandys two days earlier, it had even been agreed that the Jordanian government should be advised of the precise terms in which to make its request for military assistance![49]

Unfortunately for Macmillan, the British intervention in Jordan did not serve to prime the pump for broader Anglo-American action throughout the region. His hope that the Jordan operation would be 'part of a joint Anglo-American plan for the whole Middle East area' was not to be realised.[50] Nor even would the Americans come directly to Britain's assistance in Jordan with ground troops, despite Macmillan's pleas. Dulles described the British position as 'foolishly exposed' and in truth, it seems that Macmillan quickly came to realise this himself.[51] At any rate, he soon began to scale down his rhetoric regarding the operation in communications with the Americans. Having 'started on this difficult road', he told the President, 'I do not see how we can withdraw until we have restored stability and strength in at least some areas of the Middle East.'[52] Unfortunately for Macmillan's peace of mind over the course of the next two months, however, the US administration persisted in their estimation that the British position in Jordan was not such an area of stability and strength.[53] The fact that Macmillan managed to extricate British forces without serious trouble is more of a tribute to the comparative calm of the situation in that country than to the success of any Anglo-American regionwide operation.

The situation was calmed at least in part because of the swift emergence of a rivalry between the new Iraqi leader Brigadier Qassem and the Egyptian leader Nasser, which led Nasser to take a more flexible line over Jordan at the United Nations. It is not surprising in view of the priority which was still being given to thwarting Nasser's designs that Macmillan's government moved swiftly to try to establish good relations with the new regime in Baghdad. As early as 18 July Macmillan was arguing that there was 'quite a chance ... from the character of the men and some of their first statements that they may turn out to be more Iraqi nationalist than Nasserite.'[54] At a special Cabinet Committee meeting on 22 July, convened to discuss future Middle East policy, it was agreed that although Britain would have to come to terms with the growth of Arab nationalism:

> Arab nationalism should not necessarily be looked upon as an indivisible movement. History had shown that Damascus and Baghdad and Cairo provided different focal points for the growth of national feeling. In the long-term, it might be possible to exploit the natural differences of outlook between the Iraqis and Egyptians. There was much to be said for establishing good relations with the new Iraqi Government and building it up as a counterpart to the power of the UAR. In brief, coming to terms with the growth of Arab nationalism did not necessarily mean the establishment of a friendly relationship with Colonel Nasser.[55]

However, two other factors rapidly came to assume importance in Macmillan's calculations on the Middle East, which were to result in a shift in strategy during the course of 1959. The first was the reliance of Brigadier Qassem on the Iraqi Communist Party as a counterweight to Nasserite influence in his country. Initially, Macmillan was much less concerned about this than the US administration. As part of the policy of befriending Qassem and thwarting Nasser's intrigues, the British Ambassador in Baghdad, Sir Michael Wright, was instructed to warn Qassem about a projected Nasserite coup against him in late November 1958.[56] US Assistant Secretary of State William Rountree expressed his 'surprise' at this action, drawing forth the laconic minute from Macmillan, 'Mr. Rountree seems easily alarmed.'[57]

However, the preoccupation of the Eisenhower administration with the communist threat in the Middle East led it to take a much more suspicious view of Qassem's flirtations with the communists, and to seek to work with Nasser to counter their influence. Rountree concluded that the US should 'work with Nasser on the Iraqi situation' whilst Eisenhower himself argued that 'Nasser could oppose Communists better than can the US in the three-cornered struggle of the Middle East.'[58]

Although the balance of British policy remained different from that of the US in relation to Iraq throughout 1959, manifested in the British decision to sell Qassem arms, the growth of communist influence did present something of a dilemma. As a meeting of senior ministers at 10 Downing Street noted:

> The question arises as to whether a Communist controlled Iraq would be more inimical to our interests than a Nasserite controlled Iraq, the point being that against a Communist controlled Iraq American help could be rallied, and perhaps the whole Arab nationalist movement turned into a patriotic anti-Communist feeling. On the other hand, Nasserism and Arab Nationalism may well threaten our interests in Kuwait ...'[59]

Although the implication of the discussion was that Britain might actually be better placed to secure US assistance in the Gulf if the communists were to gain the upper hand in Iraq, either a communist or a Nasserite takeover would be perilous from a British point of view. The discussion also highlights the other reason why the Macmillan government was so concerned with developments in Iraq, and the second factor which was to bring about a change in British strategy – the position of Kuwait.

As early as the morning of 15 July 1958, Dulles was explaining the British desire to conduct wide-ranging operations to retrieve the situation in Iraq in terms of their 'tremendous investment in oil there and in nearby Kuwait'.[60] The overthrow of the Hashemite regime in Baghdad not only undercut Macmillan's strategy of relying on the Iraqi alliance to maintain British political influence in the Middle East, it called into question the security of Kuwait. Kuwait was of particular significance to the British economy at this stage, both because it was the largest producer of oil in the region, and because it was a source of oil which could be paid for in sterling. At a stroke therefore, the murder of King Feisal II had destroyed the Baghdad Pact as a means of guaranteeing British interests in the Middle East, and created a possible threat to British oil supplies from Kuwait.

Although it took some time for the impact of these changes to be digested, they began to manifest themselves in discussions of policy during the course of 1959.

THE MIDDLE EAST DOWN THE AGENDA, 1959–63

One aspect of the July 1958 operations which had been more encouraging from Macmillan's point of view, had been the willingness of the US Administration to cooperate in the defence of the Persian Gulf, where both countries had substantial oil interests, the American interest of course being principally in Saudi Arabia. A working group had been set up to discuss the coordination of plans for military operations in the area.[61] During the course of 1959, Macmillan took a particular interest in the activities of the planning group. Initially, the results were a little disappointing. Planning took some time to get started and all that was produced at first were separate British and American plans. In the middle of May, Macmillan intervened personally with Eisenhower, arguing that the time had come to turn general studies into joint plans.[62] Macmillan's aim, as he expressed it to the Cabinet Defence Committee two months later, was 'to lead the US authorities by stages to be prepared to participate in joint operations in the Middle East, particularly in Kuwait and Iraq.'[63]

Although the initiative breathed more life into the planning process, the US Joint Chiefs of Staff stuck to their original insistence that 'US military planning and operations with the UK should be on the basis of coordination as distinguished from combined or joint plans and operations.'[64] Even the persuasive skills of Chief of the Defence Staff Mountbatten could not progress matters much further in Washington.[65] In September 1959 he reported to the Cabinet Defence Committee that agreement had been reached only to exchange national plans, which might then be revised in the light of the intentions of the other party, and the facilities which each might make available to the other.[66]

After this, the question of joint planning in the Gulf and policy towards Iraq and Kuwait seems to have dropped well down the agenda of the government during the later months of 1959 and the whole of 1960. Certainly, Macmillan did not concern himself much with these issues during this period. The only development of note in what was otherwise a quiet period in the Middle East from the point of view of British policy was the beginnings of a *détente* with Nasser. This may well seem surprising in view of the thrust of Macmillan's policy since before Suez, but, as has been indicated, the Iraqi revolution had brought about some significant shifts in British strategy in the region. If Iraq were to present any threat to British interests in the Gulf, then it might be worth at least having channels of communication open to the rival regime in Cairo.

The first evidence of the *détente* comes in a memorandum from Selwyn Lloyd to Macmillan in late May 1959 in which he argued that 'it seems as though Colonel Nasser and his colleagues are prepared to think again about their future relationship with this country. Although I still fundamentally distrust him, I think it is wholly to our advantage to procure a *détente* in our relations...' This might also reflect itself in a greater willingness on the part of the Egyptian government to consider outstanding British claims for compensation in respect of the nationalisation of the Suez Canal. Macmillan approved the approach, although he stressed that it should be 'simple and short, not complicated ideas'.[67]

In the event, the restoration of diplomatic relations was to prove rather a long haul. Although chargés d'affaires were exchanged on 1 December 1959, it was not until 26 January 1961 that Harold Beeley, the new British Ambassador, presented his credentials in Cairo. In the meantime, although Macmillan had met Nasser twice at the United Nations in New York in September and October 1960, relations between the two governments had been subject to periodic bouts of recrimination which had held up the exchange of ambassadors. These reflected the depth of suspicion between the two sides. Still, in the end, the changed strategic realities of the region drove forward the process.

It was around the time of the exchange of ambassadors with the UAR that concerns about the position of Kuwait began to increase again in London. These were occasioned in the first instance by the pressure from the Ruler of Kuwait for a modification of the 1899 Agreement by which Britain had established her 'protection' over the emirate. Although it was recognised in London that this pressure could not be resisted indefinitely, the position of an independent Kuwait in relation to her powerful northern neighbour Iraq was a matter of much concern.[68] Macmillan's interest in the Middle East, which seems to have flagged somewhat after collapse of the Iraqi alliance and with it his grand plans for the region, was revived by the Kuwaiti question.

Negotiations for the independence of the emirate progressed during the early months of 1961 alongside consideration in London of the contingency of an Iraqi attack on Kuwait. The thrust of military advice, however, was very much that if an operation were to be undertaken to defend Kuwait, it would be very much better from every point of view if this could be pre-emptive. The forces required to defend Kuwait given notice of four days or more of an Iraqi attack would be far fewer than those required to dislodge Iraq from the emirate if an occupation had already taken place. In the latter case, it would be very probable that the objective could only be achieved with substantial American assistance, which could not be taken for granted.[69]

In the event, the exchange of notes between the British government and the Ruler of Kuwait of 19 June 1961 terminated the 1899 Agreement affording protection, but with the proviso that 'nothing in these conclusions shall affect the readiness of Her Majesty's Government to assist the Government of Kuwait if the latter request such assistance.'[70] The announcement of the new agreement provoked a furious response from the Iraqi leader Qassem. Radio Baghdad broadcast its condemnation and asserted that Kuwait was part of Iraq. At first it appeared unclear to Sir Humphrey Trevelyan, the British Ambassador in Baghdad, whether the Iraqi rhetoric was the prelude to military action.[71] However, he was soon suggesting that Qassem's outrage may have been fuelled by the fact that the Anglo-Kuwaiti agreement scotched an existing plan to invade Kuwait under cover of the 14 July celebrations in Iraq.[72]

The problem for the Macmillan government in all of this was that in order to defend Kuwait effectively and economically, it needed notice of an Iraqi attack so that forces could be deployed pre-emptively. In these circumstances, it took little more than a reasonably firm suspicion that Qassem might intend to invade to provoke intervention. On 29 June the government informed the Ruler of Kuwait as to its suspicions regarding Iraqi intentions, and sought an advance request for assistance should this be required.[73] Washington was also kept closely in touch with developments.[74] Significantly, in view of the attempts which both Britain and America had made to exclude France from action in the Lebanon, an area of traditional French influence, in 1958 Macmillan sent a personal telegram to President de Gaulle on the subject of Kuwait.[75] To be sure, the French had an interest in the Iraqi Petroleum Company, but one suspects that other considerations lay behind Macmillan's epistle to his 'dear friend' in the new era of Anglo-French negotiations over the EEC.

On 1 July, the Cabinet Defence Committee with Macmillan in the chair decided that the threat from Iraq was sufficient to launch the so-called operation 'Vantage' in defence of Kuwait.[76] Although conspiracy theories have since abounded as to whether the threat from Iraq was concocted purely to make a point about continuing British determination to protect her friends in the Gulf, the documents now available in British records do not lend any substance to these claims. What is most important is not whether the threat was imminent in reality, but whether Macmillan and his colleagues on the Defence Committee believed it to be so. The evidence of their discussions suggests that this was the case.[77] The US administration also, in contrast to its reaction to the Jordan intervention in July 1958, appears to have been less suspicious of British actions, although Secretary of State Rusk's questioning of Foreign Secretary Home the following month suggests some lingering doubts.[78] Nevertheless, during the vital early stages of the operation, the US was supportive, offering the assistance of a small naval combat group which was close to the area.[79] In the event, this was not needed.

Although the British government was initially much preoccupied with the question of how it would negotiate its way out of Kuwait without a recurrence of the Iraqi threat, decisive action by the Arab League in setting up a peacekeeping force eased the predicament. Throughout the crisis, however, there is a sense that Macmillan was much less excited about the possibilities of the situation than had been the case over Jordan three years earlier, or Suez two years before that. There were no more suggestions of broad Anglo-American operations sweeping throughout the region, or of British ministers returning to the role of arbiters of the fate of nations in the Middle East. Strategic realities appear to have caught up with his thinking. Instead, he confined himself to warnings on the cost of operations, albeit with a due sense of propriety for local customs. As he told Home in mid August, 'I know it is bad manners to talk about money with Sheikhs, but at some point we must raise the question of a contribution by the Sheikh to our very heavy expenses.'[80]

Still, the intervention in Kuwait had at least evidenced the importance which Macmillan continued to attach to defending British interests in the Persian Gulf. A key element in this strategy was the British base at Aden. Consequently, the outbreak of civil war in neighbouring Yemen in September 1962 between the royalist forces of the Imam and revolutionary republican forces drew the Prime Minister's attention back to the region. It also revived the simmering dislike and mistrust of Nasser which had persisted, despite the restoration of diplomatic relations. Nasser intervened in substantial force in support of the republican side which was seen as hostile to the British position in Aden. Something of an Anglo-American rift developed over the issue, with the Kennedy administration, recognising the republican regime in the face of British reluctance in December 1962.[81] The civil conflict remained unresolved when Macmillan left office although the Anglo-American rift had at least been healed by a shift in US policy against the republican side.[82]

Out of office, Macmillan remained committed to a British presence in the Gulf and was very critical of the Labour government's decision to abandon East of Suez in 1966. Whilst other parts of the Empire might be dismantled, the economic significance of the Gulf to Macmillan's mind made it one area in which Britain must continue to exert an influence. His attitude here may well shed some broader light on his attitude to decolonisation. His desire to hold on in the Gulf underlines the primacy of economic considerations in this process, despite all of the fair words spoken about the need to foster democracy around the world.

That said, however, he had presided over significant shifts in the British position in the Middle East, which had been mirrored to some degree in his own outlook. The extravagant plans of Suez in 1956 and the hopes for an Anglo-American operation to 'rectify' the situation in the Middle East in 1958 had come to nothing. The collapse of the Hashemite regime in Iraq had left Britain without a reliable regional ally and forced her to concentrate her attention on defending key positions around the Gulf. The man who had cast for Britain the role of Napoleon bursting onto the plains of Italy was forced instead to canvass sheikhs for money to support small-scale operations, albeit with the utmost sense of propriety.

NOTES

1. D. Carlton, *Britain and the Suez Crisis* (Oxford: Blackwell, 1988), p. 46.
2. Memorandum by Bevin, 25 August 1949, PRO: CAB129/36.
3. Prime Minister's visit to Washington, 30 January 1956, PRO: PREM11/1334.
4. A. Horne, *Macmillan Volume 1, 1894–1956* (London: Macmillan, 1988), p. 328.
5. Horne, *Macmillan Volume 1*, p. 367.
6. N.J. Ashton, 'The hijacking of a pact: the formation of the Baghdad pact and Anglo-American tensions in the Middle East,

1955–1958, *Review of International Studies*, Vol. 19, No. 2, April 1993, p. 131.

7. Macmillan–Foreign Office, 28 October 1955, PRO: PREM11/1033.
8. Meeting between Dulles and Macmillan in Geneva, 9 November 1955, *Foreign Relations of the United States* (Washington, 1990), (hereafter *FRUS*), p. 722.
9. Meeting between Dulles and Macmillan in Geneva, 28 October 1955, *FRUS*, p. 670. It is unclear whether this is a record of the same conversation cited in Macmillan's telegram of 28 October 1955 above. The time of the meeting in the US record is given as 11.15 a.m. on 28 October, whereas the despatch time of Macmillan's telegram cited above is recorded at 4.10 a.m. However, a complete search of US records of conversations between the two men during this period reveals no other mention of Jordanian entry into the Baghdad Pact being raised.
10. W.S. Lucas, *Divided We Stand* (London: Hodder & Stoughton, 1991), p. 75. It should be noted also that Macmillan was able to capitalise on the enthusiasm of the Turkish government for extending the pact, and to present himself as the reluctant acquiescer in Turkish plans. K. Kyle, *Suez* (London: Weidenfeld & Nicolson, 1991), p. 90 puts a rather different gloss on this.
11. Horne, *Macmillan Volume 1*, p. 422.
12. Kyle, *Suez*, p. 91.
13. Horne, *Macmillan Volume 1*, p. 397; Kyle, *Suez*, p. 155.
14. Horne, *Macmillan Volume 1*, p. 398.
15. Horne, *Macmillan Volume 1*, p. 400–1.
16. Record of a meeting held at 11 Downing Street, 3 August 1956, PRO: CAB134/1217.
17. Lucas, *Divided We Stand*, p. 161.
18. Kyle, *Suez*, p. 203.
19. H. Macmillan, *Riding the Storm 1956–1959* (London: Macmillan, 1971), p. 112.
20. Horne, *Macmillan Volume 1*, p. 423.
21. Horne, *Macmillan Volume 1*, p. 429.
22. Kyle, *Suez*, p. 464.
23. R. Rhodes James, *Anthony Eden* (London: Weidenfeld & Nicolson, 1986), p. 573.
24. Lucas, *Divided We Stand*, p. 324.
25. Carlton, *Britain and Suez Crisis*, p. 31.
26. Kyle, *Suez*, p. 534.
27. D.D. Eisenhower, *The White House Years, Waging Peace* (London: Heinemann, 1965), p. 122; Eisenhower's diary entry 21 March 1957, *FRUS*, XVII, pp. 461–2.
28. Memorandum of a conversation between Dulles, Rountree and the Ambassadors of Turkey, Iran, Iraq and Pakistan, US State Department, 780.5/12–456.

29. Record of a conversation between Selwyn Lloyd and Dulles, 10 December 1956, PRO: FO371/129327.
30. C.V. Crabb. *The Doctrines of American Foreign Policy: Their Meaning, Role and Future* (London: Lousiana State University Press, 1982), p. 164. For the alternative courses of action which Dulles was considering see Memorandum of a conversation with Senator Knowland, 8 December 1956, Eisenhower Papers, John Foster Dulles, General Correspondence.
31. Eisenhower–Dulles, 12 December 1956, Eisenhower Papers, Ann Whitman File, Dulles-Herter Series.
32. Compare 'Long Range Policy toward Egypt', undated, Bermuda briefing paper, Eisenhower Papers, White House Central File, Confidential Series, Subject Subseries; and 'Draft outline for the Prime Minister's speech at Bermuda on the Middle East', 16 March 1957, PRO:FO371/127755.
33. Plenary meeting of the Bermuda Conference, 21 March 1957, PRO:FO371/127755.
34. Lloyd–Caccia, 25 January 1957, PRO: FO371/127813.
35. Meeting between Eisenhower and Twining, 15 July 1958, Eisenhower Papers, Ann Whitman File, DDE Diary Series.
36. References to the Working Group are very sparse in both British and American documents so far released. This is no doubt due to the extreme secrecy in which it worked, and the sensitivity of the US administration in particular to its discovery. The first mention of the Group comes in a telegram from Selwyn Lloyd to Macmillan, 17 September 1957, PRO: FO371/128228.
37. Macmillan–Eisenhower, 10 October 1957, PRO: PREM11/2461.
38. Cabinet Conclusions, 27 August 1957, 'Syria', PRO: CAB128/31 Part 2.
39. A. Horne, *Macmillan Volume 2, 1957–1986* (London: Macmillan, 1989), p. 44.
40. *FRUS* 1955–57, XIII, pp. 744–7.
41. Report of a press conference given by Dulles, 10 April 1958, PRO: FO371/133799. See annotated comments of officials such as: 'Dulles sounds as though he is looking down the wrong end of a telescope to a Nasser far far away who seems to be quite happy with the Americans. You can't actually see the un-American look on his face at that distance.'
42. N.J. Ashton, ' "A Great New Venture"? – Anglo-American cooperation in the Middle East and the response to the Iraqi revolution, July 1958', *Diplomacy and Statecraft*, Vol. 4, No. 1, March 1993, pp. 62–5.
43. Lodge–Dulles, 21 May 1958, Eisenhower Papers, John Foster Dulles, Telephone Calls Series.
44. Mason–Lloyd, 21 June 1958, PRO: PREM11/2387.
45. Lodge–Dulles, 21 May 1958, Eisenhower Papers, John Foster Dulles, Telephone Calls Series.

46. Eisenhower–Macmillan, telephone conversation, 14 July 1958, PRO: PREM11/2387.
47. Meeting between Eisenhower and Twining, 15 July 1958, Eisenhower Papers, Ann Whitman File, DDE Diary Series.
48. Ashton, '"A Great New Venture"?', pp. 75–6.
49. Meeting between Macmillan, Sandys and the Chiefs of Staff, 15 July 1958, PRO: PREM11/2380.
50. Ibid.
51. Vorys–Dulles, 23 July 1958, Eisenhower Papers, John Foster Dulles, Telephone Calls Series.
52. Macmillan–Eisenhower, 17 July, 1958, PRO: PREM11/2380.
53. Foster Dulles' comments, conference with the President 23 July 1958, Eisenhower Papers, Ann Whitman File, DDE Diary Series.
54. Macmillan–Lloyd, 18 July 1958, PRO: PREM11/2408.
55. GEN 658, 1st meeting, 22 July, 1958, PRO: CAB130/153.
56. Stevens–Lloyd, 29 November, 1958, PRO: FO371/133074.
57. Macmillan's annotation, conversation between Stevens and Rountree at Heathrow Airport, 20 December, 1958, PRO: PREM11/2396.
58. Conference with the President, 23 December 1958, Eisenhower Papers, White House Office, Office of the Staff Secretary, State Department Series.
59. Meeting of ministers, 21 December 1958, PRO: PREM11/2735.
60. Dulles–Eisenhower, telephone call, 15 July 1958, Eisenhower Papers, Ann Whitman File, DDE, Diary Series.
61. Dulles–London, US State Department 780.00/7-1758.
62. Macmillan–Eisenhower, 14 May 1959, PRO: PREM11/3427.
63. 'Anglo-American Planning in the Middle East', 25 July 1959, PRO: CAB131/21.
64. JCS–Holloway, 23 August 1958, JCS Central Decimal File, 'US/UK Planning', CCS381 EMMEA.
65. Mountbatten reported considerable resistance amongst the US military to progressing the planning process during his visit to Washington. (Mountbatten–MOD, 31 August 1959, PRO: PREM11/2753).
66. Cabinet Defence Committee, 10th meeting, 18 September 1959, 'Anglo-American Planning in the Middle East', PRO: CAB131/21.
67. Lloyd–Macmillan, 25 May 1959, PRO PREM11/3266, Macmillan's comment is annotated on a de Zulueta analysis of the Foreign Secretary's memorandum, also dated 25 May 1959.
68. Watkinson–Home, 17 January 1961, and Home–Watkinson, 8 February 1961, PRO: PREM11/3427.
69. Home–Watkinson, 8 February 1961, PRO: PREM11/3427.
70. Exchange of Notes regarding relations between the United Kingdom of Great Britain and Northern Ireland and the State of Kuwait, 19 June 1961, PRO: PREM11/3427.
71. Trevelyan–FO, 26 June 1961, PRO: PREM11/3427.

72. Trevelyan–FO, 27 June 1961, PRO: PREM11/3427.
73. Home–Kuwait, 29 June 1961, PRO: PREM11/3427.
74. Home–Rusk, 29 June 1961, PRO: PREM11/3427.
75. Macmillan–de Gaulle, 30 June 1961, PRO: PREM11/3427.
76. Cabinet Defence Committee, special meeting, 1 July 1961, PRO: CAB131/26.
77. Cabinet Defence Committee, subsequent meetings, 1–4 July 1961, PRO: CAB131/26.
78. Extract from a conversation between Home and Rusk at Bougival, 6 August 1961, PRO: PREM11/3429.
79. Caccia-FO, 1 July 1961, PRO: PREM11/3428.
80. Macmillan–Home, 12 August 1961, PRO: PREM11/3429.
81. Cabinet Conclusions, 'Yemen', 20 December 1962, PRO: CAB128/36 Part 2.
82. Horne, *Macmillan Volume 2*, pp. 420–1.

4 Macmillan and British Defence Policy

Simon J. Ball

INTRODUCTION

British defence policy in the late 1950s was inextricably linked with the foreign policy objective of preserving Britain's standing as a world power. Between 1957 and 1960 the Macmillan government found several military expedients which delayed fundamental re-examination of the world role. The purpose of this chapter is to explore how the relationship between Harold Macmillan and the defence establishment made these expedients seem plausible. It concentrates on three: the elimination of air defence, the substitution of nuclear weapons for conventional arms and the substitution of American for British missile technology, and argues that Macmillan became a reformer in each area in order to pursue the conservative goal of preserving Britain's global military role.

AIR DEFENCE

In January 1957 Macmillan believed that there was egregious waste contained in the defence budget. In terms of expenditure the problem was not Britain's world role and the multiplicity of responsibilities it brought but the excess of pointless military capabilities. The manned fighter was central to Macmillan's concerns for the defence budget. It is traditional to trace his close interest in defence reform to his brief spell as Minister of Defence in 1954–55 but as early as 1950 Macmillan firmly believed that not only was there was no defence against V-2 type ballistic missiles but that an air defence system based upon the 1940 model of radar-directed fighters would be unable to intercept enough modern types of bomber to make a real difference to the survival of Britain.[1] This was a consistent theme in his later career. In August 1955 he told Rab Butler that 'it has now become quite clear that there is really no protection against a nuclear attack, certainly in these islands. The only protection is the deterrent of the counter-attack. What then is the purpose of spending these immense sums [on conventional defence]?' His well-known comment to Eden that 'it is defence expenditure which has broken our backs. We also know we get no defence from the defence expenditure' referred explicitly to the manned fighter force.[2] In Duncan Sandys, Macmillan chose a Minister of Defence who fully shared his beliefs on this issue. Sandys' wartime experience had been of the counter-V-weapon campaign. He saw no role for manned fighters in modern warfare. In March 1957 Sandys cancelled the OR329 which was to have been the fighter aircraft of the 1970s.[3] The April Defence White Paper cast doubt upon the future role of manned aircraft and simply repeated the formula for the role of air defence worked out in 1955 and 1956: fighters and missiles were to undertake the 'feasible task' of defending nuclear bomber bases.[4] Yet Macmillan and Sandys were determined to abandon air defence from January 1957. Over air defence Macmillan was willing to trim his policy for public relations reasons but not to alter it.

A fundamental problem for British defence policy in the nuclear era was the provision of a sensible defence from weapons of mass destruction for a small island close to continental Europe. Nevertheless, air defence had been ranked ahead of the independent nuclear force until the early 1950s. This trend in defence planning was strengthened by the Korean rearmament programmes of 1951–52. It was decided to order equipment which would be available in the short term, including fighter aircraft, 'off the drawing broad'. These decisions resulted in technical disasters such as the Supermarine Swift fighter[5] and distorted the defence budget to such an extent that Macmillan had to preside over a politically embarrassing special White Paper in 1955 explaining the shortcomings of the fighter programme.[6] The development of thermonuclear weapons completely undermined the idea of protecting Britain from devastation. The Strath Report of February 1955 concluded that ten hydrogen bombs dropped on urban centres would completely cripple Britain, causing 12 million fatalities and the breakdown of the social and political system.[7] Instead the advocates of air defence developed the doctrine that although no air defence system could prevent the devastation of the United Kingdom in a nuclear war such a system was essential to make deterrence credible because it would protect nuclear air bases.

Macmillan was the prime mover of the 1956 defence policy review which moved towards the position that the fighter force should be reduced to 280 aircraft by 1963 and to 200 once an effective surface-to-air guided weapons system was constructed.[8] By 1957 Macmillan and Sandys were leading a movement of opinion which held sway everywhere except in the Air Ministry. Sandys' first official pronouncement on the matter accepted an Air Ministry plan to reduce the fighter force to 280, rather than the 200 suggested by his civil servants[9] but stressed that in the medium term the role of defending bomber bases would be taken over by surface-to-air guided weapons with nuclear warheads.[10] This position was only logical if the SAM system was to protect the nuclear force from a putative Mach 2 bomber, which the Soviet Union was believed to be developing, and provide the basis for some sort of anti-ballistic missile defence but Macmillan soon became convinced that even missile defences were pointless.

The assault on Fighter Command, although inevitable since January 1957, was not actually launched until December of that year when Sandys told his officials to produce a paper which posed the central question: would the absence of Fighter Command materially increase the possibility of the V-bomber force being knocked out on the ground? The paper argued that in 1958 not only would the Russians not attack the United Kingdom without attacking American bases worldwide, a capability which they lacked, but that their preparations would give at least 24 hours warning of an attack. With this warning-time fighters would be irrelevant. By 1962 the Russians were expected to have expanded their airfield network and bomber force and to have deployed a counter-force MRBM whose 'mobility... would enable them to be deployed without any extensive site preparation' thus creating the risk of a surprise attack. The Ministry of Defence's solution to this problem was increased readiness and dispersal of the V-bomber force. They concluded that Fighter Command was militarily useless. Sandys' officials argued that, although Fighter Command defended American air bases in Britain, the Americans would not object to its withdrawal if the British government ruled it pointless for its own bases. The officials assigned only two roles to a truncated fighter force: the air defence of overseas bases in limited war and the interception of peacetime Soviet reconnaissance missions over the United Kingdom. Although the Ministry of Defence acknowledged that the same arguments could be used against SAGWs as were used against manned fighters it maintained that development must continue even if there was no large-scale operational deployment; SAGWs held out the only hope of intercepting a powered bomb launched from a bomber or creating an ABM defence.[11]

When the matter came to the Cabinet Defence Committee Macmillan gave a balanced summing-up. He recognised that the fighters could not defend Britain against bombers and even less against missiles but acknowledged that, as a result, they would make bomber attack more difficult and that the Soviets would not then be able to send any obsolete aircraft to drop atomic weapons on Britain. He argued that if Fighter Command was going to exist it had to look good to impress the Russians, the Americans, NATO allies and the population of the United Kingdom. It would therefore need to be re-equipped with Mark 3 English Electric Lightnings. Although Peter Thorneycroft railed against the nonsense of spending £570 million on a force which everyone in the room believed to be useless, Sandys was willing to accept the maintenance of the 280-aircraft force and the production of the Lightning on the grounds that disbandment would cause international difficulties.[12] In the first round of the air defence review Macmillan and Sandys put politics ahead of strategy. Macmillan then left for Australia leaving his colleagues with the problem of devising a statement to put in the 1958 Defence White Paper which would not throw public doubt on the usefulness of a force on which hundreds of millions of pounds were to be spent.[13]

For political reasons the government ducked the fighter issue in February 1958 but politics ensured that the matter would be reviewed again in the autumn of 1958 at the insistence of the Prime Minister.[14] Air defence was very expensive. On the Air Ministry's own estimates it would cost £150 million a year as compared to £170 million for the nuclear force itself.[15] As Derick Heathcoat Amory informed his colleagues a rise of £85 million in defence expenditure in 1959, inevitable on the basis of existing programmes, would remove any of the room for manoeuvre on taxation which he needed to produce an election winning budget[16] (the 17 March 1959 budget reduced income tax by 9d. amongst other tax decreases[17]). Macmillan did not believe that it was possible to prune back the Army any further[18] so Sandys told the Air Ministry to draw up a plan for the defence of air bases by missiles alone and to retain fighters only for overseas emergency reinforcement and interception of reconnaissance aircraft.[19] The Air Staff claimed to need twelve squadrons of Lightnings (156 aircraft) armed with Red Top infra-red homing missiles: four for reconnaissance recognition, four to reinforce the Mediterranean theatre and four to reinforce East of Suez.[20] Sandys regarded this claim as overgenerous; he believed eight squadrons would be sufficient,[21] but agreed to fight for it in Cabinet.[22] Amory demanded eight rather than twelve squadrons,[23] although he recognised the need to develop the Red Top missile.[24] Once more Macmillan's caution prevailed.[25] He feared that a spectacular reduction would draw public attention and cause a more general loss of confidence in the government's defence policy.[26]

The debate about air defence, however, now went beyond the supposed redundancy of the fighter aircraft. In late 1958 the Treasury started to demand that missile defence should also be abandoned.[27] The Chancellor argued that if the defence of the deterrent had been abandoned then a missile defence system was no more use than manned fighters. He was only willing to countenance a research and development programme aimed at producing ABM defences.[28] Since 1953 deployment of air defence missiles had been planned for 1958. Although the proposed function of the missiles had changed radically over the intervening five years from the mass defence of cities[29] to the protection of V-bomber[30] and Thor missile bases,[31] two types of surface-to-air guided missile were indeed ready for deployment in 1958. The politico-military argument about the whole nature of missile defence raged around the static SAGW system, Bloodhound. In 1958 the construction of eleven Bloodhound missile sites began in the United Kingdom to protect nuclear bases[32] but this missile had severe weaknesses for its task: it had limited range, could not engage low-flying targets and had a pulse radar vulnerable to jamming.[33] The RAF wanted to institute a much more ambitious system of two types of Super Bloodhound, one with a continuous wave radar and a high-explosive warhead to intercept low-level bombers and the other with command guidance and nuclear warhead to destroy bombers and guided bombs before they came within range for thermonuclear warheads to have a devastating effect.[34] It was intended that 712 missiles would be deployed in 58 fire units – 31 conventional, 27 nuclear – on the east coast, giving some defence to London and around nuclear bases.[35] The aim was to destroy 225 of the 300 bombers it was believed would get through fighter defences.[36]

The politically sensitive issue of air defence was allowed to lie dormant in the run-up to the October 1959 general election. Since the new plans would cost over £100 million for the production of the missiles (excluding the cost of nuclear warheads) and to build the sites, Sandys spent the time preparing a new attack on the concept of air defence. Once Sandys was removed the Air Ministry launched a closely-argued attempt to resurrect the justification for a costly mixed missile/fighter air defence system in November and December 1959. Yet Sandys' departure made not one whit of difference on this issue. It was Macmillan as much as his minister who was not convinced by the argument. The Ministry of Defence and Treasury would not accept that air defence contributed to the deterrent in any way which could not be achieved by readiness and dispersal.[37] The matter was taken to a personal meeting between the Minister of Defence and the Prime Minister on 8 December 1959.[38] Macmillan and Watkinson agreed with each other, as had Macmillan and Sandys, that 'no system of air defence of the UK could ever be fully effective ... we should not over-invest in any system just to make the Russian task more difficult [since] the country could not afford all projects.'[39] Super Thunderbird (the Army's mobile missile) and the continuous wave Bloodhound were kept in the programme because they were to be used for the defence of forces overseas and held out the prospect of export orders, and the twelve-squadron Lightning force was confirmed, but it was finally decided that 'defence of our deterrent could be regarded as not, in itself, justifiable on the grounds that our strategic bases were unlikely to be attacked unless the Russians were at the same time prepared to launch operations against the United States and thus initiate global war.'[40] There was thus no future for the nuclear-headed command guidance Bloodhound or an ambitious surface-to-air missile deployment programme in the United Kingdom.

The future of the manned fighters was the most contentious public relations issue of the Sandys era. The RAF attempted to mobilise informed opinion against the view that they had no long-term role[41] and thus fully drew out the conflict between 'the brass hats and Mr. Sandys'.[42] Yet the politics of the issue only delayed policy decisions rather than changed them. The high public profile of the air defence and conscription[43] issues and the rhetorical empha-

sis on nuclear weapons played a large part in giving the
defence reforms of 1957 to 1959 their radical reputation.
Yet the changes in air defence signalled a lessening of commitment to Europe and increased emphasis on the extra-
European military role: the fighter force was only saved
because of its role outside Europe.[44]

NUCLEAR WEAPONS AND THE GLOBAL ROLE

Macmillan was the driving force behind the Policy Review
Committee which, at his insistence, examined defence policy
during 1956. The PRC was the precursor of the 1957–59
reforms but its own work was disrupted by the Suez Crisis.
One clear decision the committee did reach, however, was
that nuclear weapons would allow Britain to reduce its forces
on continental Europe.[45] This was partly an economic decision: the forces were stationed outside the sterling area and
were therefore costly in hard currency. Yet the thrust of these
proposed changes was to make British military power available for reallocation to a global role. There were elements in
the British government who wanted to challenge this global
role and they coalesced after 1958 around the Future Policy
Study Group. According to Lord Carver (a participant):

> The study group spilt into two general factions, almost
> classical Whigs and Tories: all were agreed on remaining
> on good terms with the USA and of the latter's contin-
> ued involvement in the defence of Europe. The split oc-
> curred on how our influence with the USA should be
> maintained. The Tories gave priority to our maintaining
> an active world-wide presence and influence, supported
> by armed forces; the Whigs wished to give greater empha-
> sis to our being good Europeans ... pulling in our horns
> in the Middle and Far East.[46]

On this scale Macmillan was a Tory. He wanted to reduce
Britain's military role in Europe but was constrained by the
political dangers this entailed. As he told the Defence
Committee in July 1957:

The effectiveness of the deterrent depended to large extent on maintaining the vital link with the United States and other allies in Nato. It was therefore essential that we should be able to demonstrate to the Soviet Union that we were determined to keep the sea routes across the Atlantic open and to continue to provide effective support for the North Atlantic alliance. If we reduce that support, the United States might withdraw from Europe and Nato might disintegrate.[47]

Macmillan saw no positive military role for the continental commitment. Britain would commit as little to Europe as it could get away with politically and continue to spread its forces thinly around the globe (see Table 4.1).

In order to pursue this aim the British government was instrumental in getting NATO to agree a declaratory strategy which was almost wholly reliant on nuclear weapons and then to reduce its own forces in line with that strategy. The change in strategy was achieved but the implementation of force cuts was limited by Macmillan's caveat that Britain was pursuing a political rather than a purely military policy in Europe. In response to the PRC's call for a new NATO strategic concept 'that can be interpreted in terms of lower but militarily definable force levels, and a planned and coherent Allied effort ... based mainly on the idea of a "plate glass window" or "trip wire"', the Ministry of Defence produced a new directive for SACEUR in September 1956.[48] Under Macmillan's leadership the British team at the December 1956 North Atlantic Council in Paris achieved an agreement in principle to the new strategy.[49] Although the Western Europeans were unhappy with the new approach they were willing to acquiesce to a new declaratory strategy. West Germany, which was not a member of the Council, was effectively excluded from this decision but had already initiated a restructuring of the Bundeswehr in October 1956 which placed more reliance on nuclear weapons and less on manpower.[50] The French government also made it clear that they did not intend to sustain objections to the reduction of British forces.[51] It thus seemed that Britain could reallocate

Table 4.1 Proposed deployment of British forces in 1962

Area of service	Royal Navy	Army	Royal Air Force
United Kingdom	*Home Fleet* 1 aircraft carrier 1 cruiser 6 destroyers 4 frigates 1 fast minelayer 1 destroyer/escort maintenance ship 28 submarines 2 submarine depot ships 2 submarine support ships 4 fishery protection frigates 4 coastal minesweepers 2 inshore minesweepers 1 RM commando 1 special boat squadron 1 assault squadron	*Strategic Reserve* 1 division HQ 1 parachute brigade group 3 infantry brigade groups with organic armour 1 infantry brigade group without armour support units *Northern Ireland* 1 infantry brigade *UK Garrison* 13 major units including schools, public duties, home commands and units staging	*Bomber Command* 18 medium bomber squadrons 2 long-range photographic reconnaissance squadrons 2 tanker squadrons 3 tactical medium bomber squadrons 1 medium-range photographic reconnaissance squadron 2 special duties squadrons 4 IRBM squadrons *Fighter Command* 15 all-weather fighter squadrons 5 day fighter squadrons 13 SAGW sites

Table 4.1 (continued)

Area of service	Royal Navy	Army	Royal Air Force
United Kingdom (contd)	*Extended refit, modernisation or conversion* 2 aircraft carriers 7 destroyers 9 frigates 1 minesweeping HQ ship 1 destroyer escort depot ship 11 submarines 1 submarine depot ship *Trials and training* 2 destroyers 13 frigates 2 ocean minesweepers 14 coastal minesweepers 8 inshore minesweepers 1 tank landing craft 2 fast patrol boats 5 seaward defence boats 2 submarines		*Coastal Command* 8 long-range maritime reconnaissance squadrons 1 meteorological reconnaissance squadron 2 short-range search and rescue squadrons 1 special duties squadron *Transport Command* 3 long-range transport squadrons 6 1/2 tactical transport squadrons 1 short-range transport squadron *Signals Command* 1 special duties squadron

78

Table 4.1 (continued)

Area of service	Royal Navy	Army	Royal Air Force
Europe	All ships in Home Fleet, Mediterranean Fleet, Indian Ocean area (except Persian Gulf) and certain trials and training vessels earmarked for NATO	*BAOR* 2 division HQs 1 armoured brigade group 4 infantry brigade groups supporting units *Berlin* 1 infantry brigade	*RAF Germany* 4 light bomber intruder squadrons 3 medium-range photographic reconnaissance squadrons 2 fighter reconnaissance squadrons
Mediterranean	*Mediterranean Fleet* 1 aircraft carrier 1 cruiser 6 destroyers 5 frigates 6 coastal minesweepers 1 minesweeping HQ ship 3 landing ships 1 tank landing craft 2 assault squadrons 1 destroyer/escort depot ship 4 submarines 1 submarine support ship	*Cyprus* 1 infantry brigade group *Libya* 3 major units *Malta* 1 infantry battalion *Gibraltar* 1 fortress engineer regiment 1 infantry battalion	*Middle East Air Force* 4 light bomber squadrons 1 medium-range photographic reconnaissance squadron 1 tactical transport squadron 1 short-range search and rescue squadron 1 short-range transport squadron *RAF Malta* 1 medium-range photographic reconaissance squadron

Table 4.1 (continued)

Area of service	Royal Navy	Army	Royal Air Force
Mediterranean (*contd*)	1 RM brigade HQ 2 RM commandos 1 special boat section		1 long-range maritime reconnaissance squadron
Indian Ocean area	1 aircraft carrier 1 commando carrier with 1 RM commando and 1 special boat squadron 4 carrier escort frigates 8 coastal minesweepers *Persian Gulf* 6 frigates	*Aden* 1 armoured car regiment 1 infantry battalion *Kenya* 1 strategic reserve infantry brigade group	*Aden* 2 day fighter/ground attack squadrons 1 fighter reconnaissance flight 1 long-range maritime reconnaissance squadron 2 short-range transport squadrons 1 short-range search and rescue squadron *Kenya* 1 tactical transport squadron 1 short-range transport squadron

Table 4.1 (continued)

Area of service	Royal Navy	Army	Royal Air Force
Indian Ocean area (*contd*)			*Persian Gulf* 1 short-range transport squadron
Far East	*Far East Fleet* 1 cruiser 5 destroyers 5 frigates 6 coastal minesweepers 6 inshore minesweepers 7 submarines 1 repair ship	*Hong Kong* 7 or 8 major units *Malaya/Singapore* 1 division HQ 1 Commonwealth strategic reserve infantry brigade group 2 Gurkha infantry brigade groups supporting units	*Far East Air Force* 1 day fighter/ground attack squadron 1 all-weather fighter squadron 1 light bomber squadron 1 medium-range photographic reconnaissance 1 long-range maritime reconnaissance squadron 2 tactical transport squadrons 3 short-range transport squadrons 1 short-range search and rescue squadron
South Atlantic and South Africa	4 frigates 1 ice patrol ship		
America and West Indies	4 frigates	*Caribbean* 1 infantry battalion	

Source: DEFE 4/120 Annax to JP(59)79 (Final), 9 July 1959.

its forces undisturbed[52] despite the vocal case made by General Alfred Gruenther and his successor as SACEUR, Lauris Norstad, that the 'shield forces on continental Europe should be of a size and equipped in such a way that they would remain capable of imposing a threshold between Soviet aggression and massive retaliation'.[53] Since the new directive itself made the case for anti-infiltration forces[54] the reduction of British force levels remained a politically sensitive issue between 1957 and 1961.

Sandys' plan for British forces in Europe was a reduction of BAOR to 43,000 men by 1962 and 2nd Tactical Air Force to 104 aircraft, mainly nuclear-armed Canberra bombers, by 1961.[55] Only an initial reduction of BAOR from 77,000 to 64,000 was announced in April 1957. There was a certain amount of support for the British position within the Eisenhower administration. In October 1957 Macmillan and Dulles were able to agree that 'as the cost of nuclear developments increase, there is less and less capacity, and perhaps utility, in carrying out the "shield" concept' but the Secretary of State remained concerned that British actions would undermine confidence in the 'coupling' of nuclear forces with the defence of Western Europe[56] and force France down the road of developing nuclear weapons.[57] There were thus broad political restraints imposed upon Britain by the attitude of the United States but the Macmillan government was able to announce a reduction of BAOR to 55,000 in January 1958 and to negotiate a costs agreement with West Germany, signed in May 1958, envisaging only 45,000 troops by 1961.[58]

The nuclear forces Britain intended to station in Europe to compensate for troop reductions had no military role. The British did not have any concept of limited war in Europe. As the American Embassy in London reported to Dulles:

> United Kingdom doubts nuclear weapons can be used tactically on European continent and Sandys and his senior officials think that principal benefit so-called 'tactical' nuclear weapons is to add strength to nuclear deterrent by convincing Russians Nato will not meet any

aggression with conventional weapons and that any
Communist aggression in the Nato area raises grim possibility of all-out nuclear war both on Communist spear-
heads and on Communist vitals.[59]

British government representatives were quite open in private
why they wanted to reduce their forces: 'We are a global
power. Nato, until recently, had blinkers on ... but we ... have
to think globally; we have to think of the Far East and the
Middle East as well as Nato.'[60] Although the Berlin crisis and
the election of the Kennedy administration partially thwarted
this aim by freezing the rundown of BAOR at 55,000 troops it
did seem at the end of the 1950s that, with American acquiescence, the shift from Europe overseas could be achieved.

The failure of the Macmillan government to question
Britain's global role has been variously ascribed to imperial
nostalgia, fear of Soviet infiltration and bureaucratic self-
interest.[61] Whatever the motivation there were no high-
ranking challengers to the idea of Britain as a world power
within the defence establishment. Sandys and the Chiefs of
Staff certainly clashed over the exact force requirements for
limited wars outside Europe before conscription was abol-
ished in 1957. The chiefs warned that without the manpower provided by conscription it would be impossible to
fulfil Britain's military responsibilities overseas.[62] Yet this
disagreement revolved around how Britain's global military
presence should be maintained, not whether it should be
maintained. The most important idea Sandys championed
was a global system of secure British bases rather than the
maintenance of colonial control. His main concern was to
ensure that Britain's forces were stationed in countries
which would not revoke base rights once they became independent.[63] He was, for instance, sanguine about independence for Cyprus since Britain's sovereign base rights were
preserved.[64] By the summer of 1958 consensus had
emerged[65] based on the possibilities of such bases,[66] a much
larger air transport force, carrier airpower and, most importantly, the strengthening of conventional forces overseas by
the introduction of nuclear weapons.

The issue of tactical nuclear weapons overseas threw up a different balance of forces than debates about the nuclear force in Europe. All three services wanted such weapons on the grounds that they would be necessary for use in major limited wars.[67] Outside Europe, it was argued, nuclear parity between the United States and the Soviet Union would increase the risks of such wars.[68] Although Sandys ruled that only a modest contribution should be made to the Baghdad Pact (renamed CENTO after August 1959), and SEATO and the Chiefs of Staff agreed that these organisations should in no way be regarded as analogous to NATO,[69] 'each year these alliances', in Phillip Darby's phrase, 'were brought out to justify the continued worldwide distribution in very much the same way as Nato was used to argue the case for Europe.' They formed the basis of the case that nuclear weapons could replace conventional forces.[70]

In South-East Asia plans for the conventional defence of Malaya were put in abeyance during 1956[71] In the course of the next year commanders in the region called for such plans to be abandoned since Britain and the Commonwealth could not maintain enough forces on the peninsula to thwart a Chinese attack.[72] An alternative war plan was to prevent an invasion by using nuclear weapons on the Kra Isthmus which separates Malaya and Thailand. By the time of Macmillan's visit to Australia and the Far East in early 1958 the deployment of nuclear-armed V-bombers to the region had become the 'cornerstone' of British strategy.[73] During an earlier visit in the summer of 1957 Sandys seems to have promised the Australian government that a force of nuclear-capable V-bombers would be stationed in the Far East.[74] Sandys hoped that the acquisition of nuclear capability in South-East Asia would both improve cooperation with the Americans and give Britain a more influential role by turning ANZAM into a real force within SEATO. The Defence Committee agreed with him that nuclear weapons were essential to Britain's position in the region and allotted funds for the construction of a V-bomber runway and nuclear storage facilities at Tengah in Singapore.[75]

In the Middle East nuclear weapons were seen as important for both Britain's peripheral nuclear strategy and for underpinning the Baghdad Pact. For Britain the peripheral nuclear strategy was based on the assumption that the Russians had identified nuclear bases in the United Kingdom. The more bases Britain possessed the less likely they could all be neutralised and less chance that the Soviet Union would attempt to attack the United Kingdom. There were plans to disperse V-bombers to the Middle East during periods of international tension.[76] In addition, Britain was committed to the supposed military aims of the Baghdad Pact to deter Soviet aggression in the Middle East and to protect NATO's right flank in global war. Britain did not allocate any conventional forces to the Pact but in 1957 promised to provide four squadrons of nuclear-armed Canberra bombers based in Cyprus.[77] These bombers and their nuclear weapons actually arrived in late 1961.[78] Nuclear planning had no clear links with the Pact's political aims and enjoyed little support from America or the regional members, especially after the July 1958 coup in Iraq.[79] Britain, however, continued to concentrate on the Canberra force since 'much effort [had been] devoted to persuading regional members to concentrate on the major Soviet threat … in an attempt to discourage possible dangerous thoughts about Syria, Iraq, Afghanistan and India … to avoid getting embroiled in local situations … [and] to conceal her own shortcomings in the context of global war.'[80]

In practice, of course, it proved difficult to produce realistic scenarios in which nuclear weapons had an important role[81] and the whole question of limited nuclear war was reconsidered at the end of 1959. Views ranged from that of Sir Francis Festing, the Chief of the Imperial General Staff, who 'believed that in six or seven years' time the use of nuclear weapons in limited war might be readily acceptable,[82] to those of the new Minister of Defence, Harold Watkinson, who was highly sceptical. Watkinson ruled that there was to be no planning for limited nuclear war in the Middle East or Africa, although he accepted that nuclear equipped forces should be deployed in these areas.

Planning for the use of the nuclear weapons in the event of Chinese aggression was to be continued but with due regard to the fact that such a use could trigger a thermonuclear war.[83] Yet nuclear weapons continued to legitimise the Macmillan government's policy. V-bombers were deployed to Singapore during the confrontation with Indonesia; nuclear-armed bombers were based in Cyprus until 1975.[84] Britain was already committed to its role as a nuclear weapons state. Resources would have been concentrated on nuclear rather than conventional forces even if a major withdrawal from the Far East had been agreed upon. The belief that nuclear weapons would deter limited aggression short-circuited challenges to policy based on the belief that Britain did not have the military resources to sustain a global role. Regional powers would be impressed by Britain's ability to deploy nuclear weapons. Britain did not have the power to defend the Middle East from the Soviet Union – but there would be no limited aggression in the region because the Soviets would be fearful of provoking a global war. Britain could not defend Malaya against an invasion by Chinese conventional forces but China would not attempt such an invasion because of the American nuclear threat to the mainland and Britain's ability to destroy invading forces with nuclear weapons. Such ideas no longer seemed compelling in the mid-1960s when the utility of nuclear weapons was explored in the context of NATO strategy but they did underpin the belief in East of Suez in the late 1950s when defence review was actually under way.

MISSILE TECHNOLOGY

The British nuclear force had two roles: to provide a minimum deterrent through the threat of attacking thirty[85] (reduced to ten in the early 1960s[86]) Soviet cities and to convince first the Americans and then the rest of the world that Britain was a major technological, military, strategic and political world power. In 1957 the Macmillan government decided that the strategic nuclear force would

effectively comprise 104 Mark 2 V-bombers.[87] Yet this decision was merely the culmination of a series of policy debates
stretching back to the early 1950s. The Cabinet simply had
to decide how many aircraft, which were already in an advanced stage of development, the country could afford.
Macmillan was the first Prime Minister to have to deal seriously with the much more difficult problem that the technology of war was becoming too complex and too expensive
for Britain to produce at an acceptable political and economic cost. The cutting edge of such technology in the late
1950s involved missiles. Although British missiles were preferred over American in some roles such as surface-to-air[88]
and air-to-air,[89] in the field of long-range thermonuclear delivery systems Macmillan refused to bear the cost and thus
inextricably bound Britain as a very junior technological
partner to the United States.

   In January 1957 there were two British missiles under development which could conceivably ensure that Britain
would have an effective nuclear force into the 1970s: a ballistic missile, Blue Streak, and an air-launched cruise missile
with a 1000 mile range, Blue Steel Mark 2. Macmillan was
lukewarm about both. In August 1956 the PRC had decided
to cut the military research and development budget by 33
per cent to £175 million by 1958/9 on the grounds that the
scientific and engineering resources of the country were
insufficient to meet the demands put on them by the
defence programme.[90] In February 1957 Macmillan described the best way forward for the British nuclear force as
a 'modest programme of research so we could still make a
modest contribution to the United States' [strategic missile]
development programme'. At this early stage of his prime
ministership he was aware that the United States might not
agree to a programme which would effectively mean that it
would pay for the development of missiles, supply them to
the British, allow Britain to fit her own warheads and call
the result an independent nuclear force. Political opinion
in the Cabinet was also wary of passing the 'responsibility of
the deterrent' entirely into American hands.[91] Nevertheless,
Macmillan clearly regarded Blue Steel Mk 2 and Blue

Streak as second-best solutions and preferred an alternative arrangement with the Americans.

The costs of the American missile programme were also spiralling and after the launch of Sputnik and Macmillan's visit to Washington in October 1957 the United States was at least willing to explore the possibility of harnessing British technical resources. A joint technical committee met in December 1957 to discuss the possibility of integrating air-to-ground missile projects[92] and by March 1958 the Admiralty had started initial exchanges with the United States navy about its proposed submarine-launched ballistic missile, Polaris.[93] At first it did not appear that Britain and the United States had any synergy of interests. Following the repeal of the McMahon Act in 1958 Sandys went so far as to propose the immediate cancellation of Blue Streak on the grounds that it was set to cost over £200 million to develop yet was technically inferior to American missiles. He believed that the Americans would offer Britain the designs for lightweight megaton warheads which could be fitted to an advanced Anglo-American designed missile, to the Thor missile or to Blue Steel Mk 2.[94] These hopes were dashed in September 1958 when Neil McElroy, the American Secretary of Defense, told Sandys that the United States was uninterested in developing a missile with the British and wanted to provide NATO with a strategic nuclear missile under the control of the American general, SACEUR.[95] Sandys thereupon reversed himself and called for Britain to continue its own missile development.[96] The next month, however, the USAF changed its operational requirement for an air-to-surface strategic missile[97] and in December 1958 Britain agreed to consider fitting this missile to its V-bombers.[98]

Chastened by his experience with McElroy Sandys wanted to play a waiting game: continuing the full development of Blue Steel Mk 2[99] and Blue Streak whilst exploring the possibilities of acquiring either the air-to-surface missile or Polaris. Macmillan would have none of this. In the context of his planned election-winning 1959 budget Heathcoat Amory had already launched a major assault on the Blue Streak project[100] which the Treasury believed would cost two or three times the Ministry of Defence's estimate of £200 million because of the need to house it in underground silos. He called for the abandonment of the missile 'even if this meant at some time in the 1960s we should cease to have an independent deterrent' and proposed that Polaris should be adopted as an alternative. Macmillan was unwilling to agree to Amory's radical prescription of abandoning the British nuclear force[101] but he did block anything other than turnover funding for Blue Streak Mk 2[102] and instructed Sandys to set up the British nuclear deterrent study group (BNDSG) under the chairmanship of Sir Richard Powell to study the respective merits of Blue Streak, Blue Steel Mk 2, Polaris and Skybolt.[103] Initially ministers agreed that Blue Streak should be abandoned if any replacement which met the criterion of operational independence could be found and that Polaris seemed the most attractive option. Sandys, however, did not believe that the development of the missile was well enough advanced to base the whole future of the British nuclear force upon it[104] and doubted whether it would have sufficient range for British requirements.[105] More importantly perhaps the American Chief of Naval Operations, Admiral Arleigh Burke, although happy to supply the missile to Britain in the long term did not want the British involved in Polaris development because he believed they would impede technical progress and weaken the project's position in the United States' defence budget.[106] The USAF made the opposite calculation – that British participation would make their missile impossible to cancel. As a result the Air Ministry's suggestion that the next generation of the British nuclear force should be a 'flying platform' rather than a ballistic missile gained ground.[107]

A turning point came when the Chief Scientific Adviser to the Minister of Defence, Sir Frederick Brundrett, visited the United States in January 1959 and became convinced that Britain should immediately discontinue Blue Steel Mk 2 and begin joint development of the American air-to-surface missile.[108] He managed to convince the Defence Research Policy Committee of his view[109] but a major problem remained with the missile's warhead. The USAF had chosen a lightweight warhead with a lower yield and less efficient use of fissile material than the equivalent British warhead, codenamed Red Snow. To substitute the heavy Red Snow for the American warhead would seriously degrade the missile's performance and was unacceptable to the Americans. If Britain abandoned Red Snow and made the American designed warhead in Great Britain the British nuclear weapons programme would be severely disrupted, since the fissile material to make one American warhead would make four Red Snows. It was also feared that the Americans would only turn over their warhead design if they retained joint control over any potential use.[110] The warhead issue caused doubts about the viability of the project. Brundrett thought the issue was so serious that he called for Britain to abandon any further interest in the missile.[111] In response the Air Ministry reduced their requirement for fissile material so that the American warhead could be produced in Britain without insuperable difficulty.[112] Whether this was a genuine technical reappraisal or bureaucratic manoeuvre it succeeded in engaging Sandys' full support for the American missile.[113] In November 1959 the Chiefs of Staff told the BNDSG that Blue Steel Mk 2 should be abandoned and that the American surface-to-ground strategic missile should equip the next generation of the British nuclear force.[114]

In December 1959 the BNDSG advised the newly re-elected government that the best way forward for the British nuclear force was to acquire either Polaris or Skybolt. At the same time it recommended that the development of Blue Streak should be continued 'until we are quite certain that the United States will agree to our procuring WS138A [Skybolt] or Polaris on the conditions [of compete operational independence]... referred to'. In February 1960 the Chiefs of Staff informed the government that they believed the Americans would accept this condition with regard to

Skybolt. They called for Blue Streak to be cancelled on the
grounds that its liquid-fuel system meant that it took so long
to prepare for launch that it could only be used for a pre-
emptive strike rather than launch-on-warning or second
strike. Their views were accepted by Sandys' successor
Harold Watkinson. Later in the month he presented a statement to the Defence Committee which was adopted as
formal British policy:

> We shall wish to continue to maintain under our undi-
> vided control the ability to deliver a significant number of
> megaton weapons ... it is not, however, indispensable to
> our objective that the means of delivery should be of our
> own design or manufacture, provided we can buy what we
> want without political conditions ... [and] produce our
> own nuclear warheads.[115]

This was exactly the same policy adumbrated by Macmillan
in the same committee in February 1957. Although he had
sat above the fray for most of the next three years and used
Sandys and the BNDSG to fight his battles Macmillan
achieved the aim he had set himself as early as 1956. The
key development, and Macmillan's opportunity, had been
the United States government's decision to offer Britain
Skybolt, but not Polaris, on acceptable terms. The offer was
formalised in a memorandum of understanding signed by
Thomas Gates, McElroy's successor, and Harold Watkinson
in June 1960. The United States refused to sign a govern-
ment-to-government 'contract to purchase' but promised to
continue development of the missile and the British agreed
to buy 100. Macmillan took a close interest in the memorandum of understanding and summoned Watkinson to
Birch Grove immediately on his return from the United
States for an in-depth briefing. Macmillan chose to ignore
the warnings of civilian officials at the Pentagon and the
President's scientific advisers that Skybolt was a speculative
USAF research and development project which involved
immense technical problems.[116]

At one level this was a political misjudgement. Macmillan
believed that Anglo-American relations were more import-

ant to Eisenhower and Kennedy than refining the United States defence budget. Yet the Nassau summit in December 1962 demonstrated that a President was willing to make large political concessions to Britain. More fundamentally Britain gave up any hope of an independent nuclear policy in June 1960. Nuclear weapons shifted from the realm of defence policy into the realm of international politics in mid 1960. This was Macmillan's choice. Although constrained by the economics and scientific possibilities of technological development the Prime Minister could steer the defence establishment. Once the memorandum of understanding, which was not binding on either side but left the Americans with multiple options but Britain with only one, was concluded it did not matter whether Macmillan was a reformer in defence affairs but only if he was a skilled negotiator. The Skybolt decision was like a Russian doll. The defence establishment was the visible outer face, under them was Macmillan and under him was the United States government. The decisions were effectively made in Washington.[117]

CONCLUSION

The decisions taken about nuclear missile technology illustrate Macmillan's approach well. The possession of such missiles constituted both a role and a capability. The role was Britain's as a nuclear power; the capability was the delivery of thermonuclear weapons against the most sophisticated possible enemy, the Soviet Union. Macmillan was willing to explore a new ways of achieving the capability but had no intention of challenging the role. This is in striking contrast to his hostility to air defence where he challenged the necessity of the role, the defence of the United Kingdom in the thermonuclear age, and then diminished the capability, a mixed fighter/missile force to intercept incoming bombers. Macmillan's tenacity on the air defence issue was unusual for him on a substantive strategic issue. He certainly had long-held opinions on this issue but was sustained by being part of a consensus. He only had to support Sandys and his civil ser-

vants to overcome the dissenters in the Air Ministry. Over
Britain's role as a world power, which involved numerous capabilities, Macmillan was part of the conservative consensus.
He had a number of important insights – the political role of
forces in Europe, the futility of military action outside the
American orbit and the need for some kind of colonial
retreat – but never contemplated pushing them to the logical
extent advocated by some middle-ranking civil servants and
military officers. In one sense this position was essential for
the Prime Minister's control of the Conservative party but
there is also evidence of a natural pattern of behaviour which
cut defence costs without facing the underlying problems of
Britain's world role.

NOTES

1. AIR19/662, 'Biggin Hill No Safeguard'. Speech by Macmillan at
    Hayes reported in the *Bromley and Kentish Times*, 27 October 1950.
2. A. Horne, *Macmillan Volume 1, 1894–1956* (London: Macmillan,
    1988), p. 381.
3. C. James, "The Impact of the Sandys Defence Policy on the Royal
    Air Force', *Proceedings of the Royal Air Force Historical Society*, IV
    (1988), p. 21.
4. Cmnd 124, *Defence, Outline of Future Policy.*
5. This aircraft was introduced into service as an interceptor fighter in
    February 1954 and withdrawn in May 1955.
6. Cmd 9388, *Supply of Military Aircraft.*
7. DEFE5/80, COS(57)278, Appreciation of the likely form and dura-
    tion of a future major war with special reference to the problem of
    stockpiling in the UK, 18 December 1957 (refers to earlier, still
    classified, report).
8. AIR8/2046, The Policy Review: Reply to the Minister of Defence's
    Directive of 21 December 1956: Note by Air Ministry, 10 January
    1957.
9. DEFE13/237, Sir Richard Powell to Minister of Defence, 16
    January 1957.
10. AIR19/856, Review of Defence Plans. Note by Minister of Defence,
    22 February 1957.
11. DEFE7/968, Fighter Defence of Britain. Note by Minister of
    Defence (written by Richard Way, Deputy Secretary, Ministry of
    Defence), 20 December 1957.
12. CAB131/18, D(57)14th meeting, 31 December 1957.

13. PREM11/2272, CRO Telegram Track 147. Prime Minister to Lord Privy Seal, 7 February 1958.
14. CAB131/20, D(58)35, Memorandum by the Prime Minister, 2 September 1958.
15. AIR8/2220, Assistant Chief of the Air Staff (Policy) to Chief of the Air Staff, 10 September 1958.
16. CAB131/19, D(58)24th meeting, 5 November 1958.
17. A. Horne, *Macmillan Volume 2, 1957–1986* (London: Macmillan, 1989), p. 142.
18. CAB131/19, D(58)24th meeting, 5 November 1958.
19. AIR8/2220, Richard Way to R. Kent (Assistant Under-Secretary, Air Ministry), 2 October 1958.
20. AIR8/2220, Assistant Chief of the Air Staff (Policy) to Chief of the Air Staff, 10 September 1958.
21. AIR8/2220, Richard Way to R. Kent, 29 September 1958.
22. CAB131/20, D(58)61, Memorandum by the Minister of Defence, 14 November 1958.
23. CAB131/20, D(58)69, Memorandum by the Chancellor of the Exchequer, 17 November 1958.
24. CAB131/19, D(58), 26th meeting, 18 November 1958.
25. CAB131/19, D(58), 31st meeting, 22 December 1958.
26. CAB131/19, D(58), 26th meeting, 18 November 1958.
27. CAB131/19, D(58), 24th meeting, 5 November 1958.
28. CAB131/19, D(58)69, Memorandum of the Chancellor of the Exchequer, 17 November 1958.
29. AIR19/949, AC(53)46, Progress Report on the Introduction of Surface-to-Air Guided Weapons into the Royal Air Force. Note by Deputy Chief of the Air Staff, 14 September 1953.
30. AIR19/949, AC 12(55), (Special) Top Secret Annex A, 30 June 1955.
31. AIR19/949, AC 9(58), Top Secret Annex B, 14 April 1958.
32. AIR19/949, AC(58)29, The Deployment of Stage 1 SAGW. Note by Deputy Chief of the Air Staff, 1 April 1958.
33. AIR19/949, AC 12(55), (Special) Top Secret Annex A, 30 June 1955.
34. AIR20/10805, Ministry of Defence: Defence Research Policy Committee. Surface-to-Air Guided Weapons with Nuclear Warhead. Note by Deputy Chief of the Air Staff, undated [1959].
35. DEFE7/1690, Sir Richard Powell to Sir Roger Makins (Permanent Under-Secretary, Treasury), 6 April 1959.
36. DEFE7/1690, F.W. Mottershead (Assistant Secretary, MoD) to R.C. Kent, 5 June 1959.
37. DEFE4/122, COS(59), 72th meeting, Confidential Annex, 24 November 1959.
38. DEFE4/123, COS(59), 75th meeting, 8 December 1958.
39. DEFE4/123, COS(59), 78th meeting, Confidential Annex, 22 December 1959.
40. CAB131/21, Minutes of meeting of Cabinet Defence Committee, 23 December 1959.

41. AIR8/2212, Sir Maurice Dean (Permanent Under-Secretary, Air Ministry) to Secretary of State for Air (George Ward), 20 November 1957.
42. AIR8/2212, Sir Dermot Boyle to Sir Maurice Dean, 21 October 1958.
43. M. Navias, *Nuclear Weapons and British Strategic Planning 1955–58* (Oxford: Clarendon Press 1991), pp. 91–5, 148–9 and 154–7.
44. CAB131/19, D(58), 27th Meeting, 20 November 1958.
45. James, 'The Impact of the Sandys Defence Policy on the Royal Air Force', pp. 11–14.
46. M. Carver, *Out of Step: Memoirs of Field Marshal Lord Carver* (London: Hutchinson, 1989), pp. 288–9.
47. CAB131/18, D(57), 6th meeting, 31 July 1957.
48. AIR8/2065, Minister of Defence (Sir Walter Monckton) to Chiefs of Staff, 2 September 1956.
49. Navias, *Nuclear Weapons*, pp. 51–65.
50. Beatrice Heuser and Robert O'Neill (eds), *Securing the Peace in Europe, 1945–1962* (London: Macmillan, 1992), pp. 142–4.
51. DEFE13/237, Sir Gladwyn Jebb (Ambassador in Paris) to Foreign Secretary (Selwyn Lloyd), 1 March 1957.
52. DEFE4/93, COS(56), 133rd Meeting, 18 December 1956.
53. DEFE4/92, JP(56) 162 (Final) Annex. 26 November 1956, and DEFE7/1162, Note of Minister of Defence's talk with SACEUR, 12 December 1956.
54. DCKN5/2, Directive to the NATO Military Authorities from the North Atlantic Council.
55. AIR19/856, Note by Minister of Defence, 22 February 1957.
56. Ann Whitman-Dulles/Herter papers, Box 7 October 57(1), Memorandum of a conversation at the British Embassy between the Prime Minister and the Secretary of State, 23 October 1957.
57. DEFE13/237, Note of a conversation between Sir Richard Powell and SACEUR on 2 May 1957, 6 May 1957.
58. W. Park, *Defending the West: A History of NATO* (Brighton: Wheatsheaf, 1986), p. 47.
59. Department of State Telegram No. 2972, American Embassy, London to Department of State, 9 November 1957.
60. DCKN5/10, British Aspects of Military Strategy. Lecture by Marshal of the Royal Air Force Sir William Dickson to NATO Defence College, 3 October 1958.
61. See amongst others: P. Darby, *British Defence Policy East of Suez, 1947–1968* (London: Oxford University Press, 1973), pp. 153–4 and D. Lee. *Eastward* (London: HMSO, 1984), pp. 184–5.
62. DEFE32/5, COS(57), 13th meeting, Confidential Annex, 18 February 1957.
63. AIR8/2180, Chairman, Chiefs of Staff Committee (Sir William Dickson) to Chiefs of Staff, 11 July 1957.

64. CAB131/21, D(59), 10th meeting, 18 September 1959.
65. PREM11/2639, Duncan Sandys to Prime Minister, 9 July 1958.
66. DEFE5/94, COS(58), 175, Worldwide Requirements for British Bases and Alternative Potential Bases. Memorandum for the Minister of Defence, 10 July 1958.
67. DEFE4/100, COS(57), 73rd meeting, 24 September 1957.
68. DEFE4/94, COS(58), 77th meeting, 3 September 1958.
69. DEFE4/94, COS(57), 8th meeting, 29 January 1957.
70. AIR8/2152, Chief of the Air Staff to Minister of Defence, 26 June 1957.
71. AIR8/2154, Assistant Chief of the Air Staff (Policy) and Assistant Under-Secretary (Air Staff) to Chief of the Air Staff and Secretary of State for Air, 13 November 1957.
72. AIR20/10113, Commander-in-Chief Far East Air Force to Vice-Chief of the Air Staff, 6 December 1957.
73. DEFE4/102, JP(57)168 (Final), 24 December 1957.
74. DEFE4/100, COS(57), 70th meeting, Confidential Annex, 10 September 1957.
75. CAB131/19, D(58), 3rd meeting, 20 February 1958.
76. DEFE4/116, JP(59) 17 (Final) [The military brief for Macmillan's visit to Moscow], 9 February 1959.
77. DEFE4/102, COS(57), 95th meeting, Confidential Annex, 11 December 1959.
78. D. Lee, *Wings in the Sun* (London: HMSO, 1989), p. 176.
79. DEFE4/111, JP(58), Note 28, 28 August 1958.
80. DEFE4/120, JP(59) 107 (Final), 19 August 1959.
81. DEFE7/1642, Mr Benwell to Mr Lawrence-Wilson, 14 April 1959.
82. DEFE4/121, COS(59), 65th meeting, 20 October 1959.
83. CAB131/122, D(59) 46, 24 December 1959.
84. Lee, *Wings in the Sun*, pp. 177–8.
85. DEFE4/111, COS(58), 77th meeting, 3 September 1958.
86. Sir Richard Way speaking in 1987.
87. CAB131/18, D(57), 7th meeting, 2 August 1957.
88. AIR19/949, Major-General E. Moore (Chief, Military Assistance Advisory Group – United Kingdom) to Sir Richard Powell, 13 August 1958.
89. DEFE4/113, DRP/P(58)82, 22 October 1958.
90. DEFE4/85, COS(56) 33rd meeting, 20 March 1956; AIR19/855, AC(56)85, Reductions in the Ministry of Supply's Defence Research and Development Programme to £175 million in 1958/9. Note by Deputy Chief of the Air Staff, undated.
91. CAB131/18, D(57), 2nd meeting, 27 February 1957.
92. AIR2/14711, Report of the joint USAF-RAF Task Group on Air-to-Ground Weapons. Interdependence Sub-Committee D (Delivery Systems), April 1958.
93. Navias, *Nuclear Weapons*, pp. 234–5.
94. CAB131/20, D(58)47, 8 September 1958.

95. DEFE13/180, Record of meetings held at the Pentagon and State Department, Washington DC, 22–25 September 1958, 14 October 1958.
96. CAB131/20, D(58)57, 3 November 1958.
97. AIR2/14711, Deputy Director of Operational Requirements (British Air Force Staff, Washington) to Assistant Chief of the Air Staff (Operational Requirements), 19 November 1958.
98. AIR2/14711, Strategic Air-to-Surface Missile Interdependence Short Summary. Deputy Chief of the Air Staff (Sir Geoffrey Tuttle) to Sir Frederick Brundrett, 22 December 1958.
99. AIR2/14711, Minister of Defence to Prime Minister, 30 December 1958.
100. CAB131/19, D(58), 14th meeting, 23 July 1958.
101. CAB131/19, D(58), 31st meeting, 22 December 1958.
102. AIR2/15261, Secretary of State for Air to Minister of Defence, 24 June 1959.
103. DEFE4/115, COS(59) 4th meeting, Confidential Annex, 13 January 1959.
104. CAB131/20, D(58)57, 3 November 1958.
105. DEF13/193, CWP/P(58)11, The Possibilities of Alternatives to Blue Streak, 7 May 1958.
106. J. Elliot, "The cancellation of the Blue Streak missile system and its relevance to British nuclear thinking and strategy, 1954–1960' (unpublished MPhil dissertation, Cambridge University, 1990), pp. 93–9.
107. DEFE7/991, Sir Richard Powell to Mr L.J. Sabatini, 6 January 1959.
108. AIR2/14711, Sir Frederick Brundrett to Sir Richard Powell, 3 January 1959.
109. AIR2/15261, DRP/M(59)1, 27 January 1959.
110. AIR2/15261, DRP/P(59)38, Interdependence – Strategic Air-to-Surface Weapons, 14 April 1959.
111. AIR2/15261, DRP/M(59)6, 21 April 1959.
112. AIR2/15261, Secretary of State for Air to Minister of Defence, 24 June 1959.
113. AIR2/15211, Minister of Defence to Secretary of State for Air, 14 July 1959.
114. DEFE4/122, COS(59), 72nd meeting. Confidential Annex, 24 November 1959.
115. Elliot, 'The cancellation of Blue Streak', pp. 125–7.
116. S. Zuckerman, *Monkeys, Men and Missiles* (London: Collins, 1988), pp. 237–9.
117. For accounts of American policy-making see K. Cibowski, 'The bureaucratic connection: explaining the Skybolt decision', in J. Endicott and R. Stafford (eds), *American Defense Policy* (Baltimore: Johns Hopkins University Press, 1977, 4th edn), pp. 374–88 and R. Neustadt, *Alliance Politics* (New York: Columbia University Press, 1970), Professor Neustadt's original report to Kennedy has now been declassified.

5 Macmillan and the End of the British Empire in Africa

Philip E. Hemming

When Harold Macmillan became Prime Minister in January 1957, Britain still held sway over fifteen territories in Africa; by 1964 there were only four left. Over two-thirds of British African possessions attained independence during the Macmillan government. Although decolonisation had already swept much away when Macmillan took office, Africa remained a complicated issue awaiting resolution. There was little doubt that in time Britain would divest herself of her African territories; the question was how fast she would do so and in what manner. This chapter addresses the role of Macmillan himself in the climb-down from Empire. How much influence did he have on setting the decolonisation agenda? To what degree was he affected by domestic consid-erations? What influence did other foreign policy considera-tions have on his thinking? Finally, what did he hope to achieve through decolonisation and how successfully did he fulfil his aim?

Shedding the Empire was not, in Macmillan's eyes, tantamount to surrendering Britain's status as one of the world's great powers. Former British possessions would mark their coming of age on the global scene with formal membership of the Commonwealth. As *primus inter pares* in the Commonwealth, the United Kingdom would continue to exercise a political, economic and strategic leadership role among her erstwhile territories. In this manner Britain's international importance would be maintained.

The process of African decolonisation was already well under way by the time Macmillan took office. British postwar colonial policy could be more accurately described as a decolonisation policy. From 1945, both Labour and Conservative governments recognised the need for Britain to divest herself gradually of Empire.[1] The Attlee government, with Arthur Creech-Jones as Colonial Secretary, instituted a policy of colonial economic development. This was aimed primarily at tapping African wealth to support a dangerously weak British economy.[2] Yet the lessons of Indian nationalism were also fresh in mind, as reflected in the Cohen Report of 1947 which advocated building up local government in the territories. In this manner, it was hoped that African nationalism, embryonic and inchoate as it was, could be positively channelled. This hope was soon proven ill-founded; the very amorphousness of African nationalism made it volatile. In 1948 the Gold Coast riots left 29 dead and forced Andrew Cohen into speeding up the process towards independence. This was a pattern that was to repeat itself in all African territories. The British often found themselves struggling between the twin desires of preparing their possessions slowly and adequately for independence, and of proceeding fast enough to stay one step ahead of nationalist fervour.

This policy was relatively straightforward in West Africa, where there was little European settlement. In East and Central Africa, however, the picture was complicated by the presence of a substantial white European settler population. The Europeans did not relish the prospect of independence under African majority rule and were both vocal and stubborn in their efforts to maintain paramountcy. There was much fear in Whitehall that the settlers would choose to throw in their lot with the Union of South Africa, in which case all of Britain's work in Africa 'would be undone. The policies [of apartheid] that we detest in the Union would be established ... in the heart of this part of our Colonial Empire.'[3]

To guard against this eventuality, the three territories of Northern Rhodesia, Southern Rhodesia and Nyasaland were bound together in 1953 to form the Federation of Rhodesia and Nyasaland. While its genesis was a response to the South African threat, the Federation was presented publicly as the start of a multiracial partnership that would be politically and economically beneficial to both whites and Africans in all three territories.[4] Paradoxically, it ultimately rendered the path to independence and Britain's withdrawal from Africa more tortuous; it was to become the Gordian knot of Macmillan's colonial policy. Federation ran against African sentiment and allowed the Southern Rhodesian economy to expand at the expense of the other two territories.[5] Politically, federation shored up the privileged position of the Europeans. The settlers considered the Federation indissoluble and regarded the British initiative in its creation as a promise to that effect.[6] In short, the Federation bolstered the position of the European minority and gave false promise for African advancement. This, as Prosser Gifford put it, complicated Britain's task 'of achieving an honourable extraction from British Central Africa'.[7]

This then was the legacy that Macmillan inherited upon becoming Prime Minister. For him, imperial policy – and Africa in particular – never held a special attraction; his only direct encounter had been in his position as Under-Secretary at the Colonial Office. A 1942 speech revealed his early thoughts on the Empire. He saw it not as a static, inflexible entity, but one with 'the great quality of adaptation'. The colonies, he said, 'are poor because they are just beginning. They are four or five centuries behind. Our job is to move them, to hustle them, across this great interval of time as rapidly as we can.' This tutor–student relationship between Britain and the colonies should be based on 'the principle of partnership' out of which would grow 'understanding and friendship. Within the fabric of the Commonwealth lies the future of the Colonial territories.'[8]

Macmillan carried this belief with him into office as Prime Minister. His speech delivered in July 1957 at Bedford is best known for his 'never had it so good' quip. Yet in a foreshadowing of his 1960 'winds of change' speech, he warned that nationalism, 'which a few years ago was but a ripple, has become a tidal wave surging from Asia across the ocean to the shores of Africa ... Of all political forces, the new rise of nationalism is the most powerful, swift and elemental ... It can be led: but it cannot be driven back.'[9]

Macmillan recognised that African nationalism was a force which could not be resisted. The Mau Mau insurrection in Kenya had demonstrated how costly in lives and money a counter-insurgency campaign could be. It had also shown the futility of using force to dampen nationalist uprisings. In addition, the economic advantages of the colonies were no longer significant enough to justify maintaining the Empire. As Chancellor of the Exchequer, he advocated reducing colonial development and in January 1957 commissioned a Cabinet Colonial Policy Committee report which concluded that the costs of Empire were 'fairly evenly matched' with the benefits.[10] The Empire was also losing its strategic rationale. The 1957 Defence Review stressed the importance of nuclear weaponry; maintaining costly forces for major colonial policing ran contrary to this reorientation.[11] Although East Africa was still seen as strategically vital, especially after the loss of Egypt, British access to bases rested on agreement with nationalists rather than armed occupation.[12]

The realisation of the dangers of force was reinforced by the painful French experiences in Indochina and Algeria, as well as by the Suez débâcle.[13] Suez revealed the depth of anti-colonial feeling in the international arena. The American Secretary of State John Foster Dulles regarded British action as 'the straight old-fashioned variety of colonialism of the most obvious sort', while Indian Prime Minister Jawaharlal Nehru lamented Britain's relapse into colonialism.[14] It seemed clear that any use of British troops to quell a nationalist uprising in Africa would be met with worldwide condemnation, and possibly even United Nations intervention.[15]

Macmillan was firmly convinced of the need to address the problem of Africa. He did not envisage a formal empire, foreseeing instead a steady process whereby colonies would graduate first to self-rule and then to independence, arriving on the world scene as a member of the Commonwealth. This reflected his belief that Britain held a unique position at the intersection of 'three circles' – Europe, America and the Commonwealth. By strengthening the Commonwealth circle, he sought to maintain Britain's importance in the other two.[16] In Macmillan's thinking, this could be accomplished by both the process and result of decolonisation. The process would demonstrate that Britain was an enlightened power, cognisant of the new currents sweeping across the world and able to adapt to them. The result would be an expanded Commonwealth, a family of nations sharing values of responsible government, freedom and morality, 'with an important role to play in the world struggle'.[17] In this way, Britain would maintain her global importance.

Macmillan's strength was his far-ranging intellect, which was initiating new, broad policy concepts. But when it came to working on the details, he had little patience.[18] However, his colonial policy from 1957 until 1960 was characterised by caution. In his first three years in office, Macmillan neither undertook any major initiatives in Africa, nor made any significant changes at the Colonial Office. Alan Lennox-Boyd, appointed Colonial Secretary in 1954, stayed in office. The period 1953–56 was a time of consolidation for African nationalists and was marked by 'heady progress in both political participation and the lifting of racial discrimination for a few middle-class Africans'.[19] Despite the scathing accusations of gunboat neo-colonialism following Suez, direct international pressure for decolonisation was not acute.

While the international arena was relatively quiet, the primary motivation for Macmillan's low-profile policy on Africa was the overriding need to heal the wounds inflicted by Suez on the Conservative Party.[20] Speaking to Lord Swinton, Macmillan said: 'Our first objective must be to keep the party together, at all costs united. It's like keeping five balls in the air simultaneously, knowing that we are doomed if we drop one.'[21] This juggling act involved not undertaking any initiatives that might divide the party. There was still a significant body of back-bench opinion that saw the Conservative Party as the defender of Britain's traditional global role as the head of the Empire and the (then all-white) Commonwealth. The negotiations over Cyprus, in which Macmillan had been personally involved as Foreign Secretary, had by 1957 come to a head with the right wing of the party up in arms. In March Lord Salisbury resigned as Lord President about the decision to release Archbishop Makarios, and a backbench revolt in the Commons was a real possibility. Macmillan took this threat very seriously and was both surprised and relieved when it fizzled out in August.[22] In this light, Macmillan did not feel the time was right to take any radical initiatives in Africa. The same Tory traditionalists so opposed to Macmillan's moves in Cyprus were equally ardent in their support for the European populations in Central and East Africa. Anything that could possibly be interpreted as undermining the settlers' position would undoubtedly have hardened the right-wing back-benchers and increased the chance of a revolt in Parliament.

This is not to say that Africa was completely ignored by Macmillan during his first government. As mentioned above, he commissioned the Cabinet Colonial Policy Committee report on colonial economic performance soon after entering No. 10. In 1958, a major interdepartmental reassessment of British colonial policy was initiated, culminating in a 1959 Foreign Office paper entitled 'Africa: The Next Ten Years'.[23] Macmillan himself maintained interest in the debate, minuting in July 1959 that 'African problems will undoubtedly become more important to us in the next ten years and this is one of the few parts of the world in which the European powers still have direct influence.' He went on to explain that he did not propose a hasty shift in policy, but that it was time to start thinking of the future.[24] Plans for consultations with American, French and Belgian officials were drawn up in preparation for a new African initiative. The Colonial Office greeted this development with a conservative defence of its record. Secretary of State Alan Lennox-Boyd argued that the pace and form of British colonial policy as it stood provided the best road to a stable, independent Africa.[25]

Foreign Secretary Selwyn Lloyd applauded the proposed consultations, minuting that a 'full and frank' exchange of views would be beneficial.[26] Yet all of this debate was akin to the proverbial duck swimming in a pond: outwardly tranquil with much activity under the surface.

In 1959 two crises within British territories finally forced Macmillan to confront the issue of African decolonisation more decisively: the Hola camp massacre and the Devlin Report on the Nyasaland riots. In March, eleven of the thousand 'hard-core' Mau Mau rebels still incarcerated were beaten to death at the Hola detention camp in Kenya. An inquiry was set up and the resulting White Paper, issued in June, condemned the lack of oversight at the camp. Following the return of the Nyasaland Congress leader Dr Hastings Banda, African nationalists embarked on a campaign of disorder and sabotage in protest against repressive Southern Rhodesian policies. Fifty-two Africans were killed, many were detained, Banda was imprisoned in Salisbury, and Federal authorities imposed a state of emergency. The Cabinet authorised a formal inquiry, which resulted in the Devlin Report. Released in July, it accused the colonial administration of running a 'police state'.[27]

These two incidents threatened trouble in Parliament at a politically delicate time. Macmillan later commented that with a General Election looming, all seemed calm 'with the exception of the African troubles'. The Commons debate the following the Hola massacre was fraught, and Lennox-Boyd offered to resign twice within a month. On both occasions Macmillan refused to accept, primarily because it would 'be a great blow to Her Majesty's Government at the most critical period before the General Election, when all is going well otherwise'.[28] Julian Amery and Lord Perth seemed likely to follow Lennox-Boyd were he to leave, thus compounding the danger. A Cabinet meeting in July endorsed Macmillan's support of his Colonial Secretary, and the Prime Minister informed the ministers present that if any other decision had been reached, he would not have continued in office.[29] The whole issue was trivialised and, denied the light of publicity, quickly faded.

The events of 1959 convinced Macmillan that the time had come to take the initiative in Africa. However, it was imperative that any such step did not threaten Tory chances for an election victory. With this in mind, Macmillan took three well-timed steps to put Africa on the political agenda. The first was to create a Royal Commission under Sir Walter Monckton tasked with investigating and reporting on the viability of the Federation prior to the Constitutional Conference set for 1960. Despite heated opposition from Sir Roy Welensky, the volatile European Prime Minister of the Federation, Macmillan was determined to send the Commission as 'African opinion is all the time being inflamed'.[30] In his brief to Monckton, he revealed his assessment of the problem:

> [I]f we fail in Central Africa to devise something like a workable multi-racial state, then Kenya will go too and Africa may become no longer a source of pride or profit to the Europeans who developed it, but a maelstrom of trouble into which all of us will be sucked ... The cruder concepts, whether of the left or of the right, are clearly wrong. The Africans cannot be dominated permanently ... Nor can the Europeans be abandoned.[31]

In this statement, one can see the two strands that characterised Macmillan's approach to the problem of Africa. On the one hand, he was aware of the dangers of foot-dragging: vacillation could well result in a drawn-out, painful colonial war. On the other hand, Macmillan's commitment to 'the middle way' cautioned him against moving too quickly. The problem was reconciling the two.

With the General Election over the Conservatives returned to power with an overwhelming majority. Macmillan felt ready to tackle the problems of Africa. On 1 November, he made the decision to visit Africa in the New Year, writing: 'Something must be done to lift Africa on to a more national plane, as a problem to the solution of which we must all contribute ... by some really imaginative effort.'[32] Such a grand gesture certainly appealed to Macmillan's penchant for dramatic statesmanship. The African tour lasted six weeks and encompassed Nigeria, Ghana, the Central African Federation and South Africa. In Cape Town, he delivered his now famous 'winds of change' speech. Aimed primarily at the Afrikaners in South Africa and the European settlers in the Federation, it declared: 'The wind of change is blowing through this continent, and, whether we like it or not, this growth of national consciousness is a political fact. We must all accept it as a fact, and our national policies must take account of it.'[33]

Tim Bligh, Macmillan's Private Secretary, had been hinting throughout the trip that 'something was cooking which would astonish and satisfy us all'; this apparently was it.[34] Criticism was levelled at the speech's lack of originality, but it was nevertheless a *tour de force* that underlined the Prime Minister's dedication to independence for British African territories sooner rather than later.

Macmillan's third – and decisive – step was the appointment of Iain Macleod as Colonial Secretary following the General Election. Macleod, a passionate, committed liberal Tory, courageously and skilfully engineered the withdrawal of Britain from a majority of its remaining African territories. He was not afraid of confronting the hard details, and was therefore the perfect complement to Macmillan's 'grand policy sweep' approach. Macleod also served as a lightning-rod in Parliament, bearing the brunt of opposition to change in Africa. By the time he was forced to resign by the right wing of the Conservative Party, he had already prepared most of British African possessions for independence. 'It has been said', Macleod later wrote, 'that after I became Colonial Secretary there was a deliberate speeding up of the movement towards independence. I agree. There was. And in my view any other policy would have led to terrible bloodshed in Africa.'[35]

Between 1959 and 1962, Macleod built an impressive record at the Colonial Office. Starting with Kenya, he recognised the need to untie the knot of African nationalism and settler recalcitrance. Though keen to speed up the pace of decolonisation, he was mindful of the need to treat the Kenyan situation carefully. At the January 1960 constitutional conference, Macleod announced that majority rule had to be recognised. African and European leaders agreed on a constitution and elections were held in early 1961. Macmillan feared a 'big problem' at home, with Lord Salisbury – a champion of white settlers' rights – possibly staging a party revolt. At issue was the future of Jomo Kenyatta, the imprisoned leader of the KANU party, widely held responsible for Mau Mau. Macmillan realised that 'Kenya without Kenyatta was like Hamlet without the Prince of Denmark', and Macleod handled the African leader masterfully, gradually lifting restrictions on his movements and activities.[36]

Tanganyika was the British territory that was least prepared for independence. While economically and educationally underdeveloped, it nevertheless had strong political leadership in the form of Julius Nyerere and his TANU party. In the spring of 1960, Macleod met with Nyerere at the former's London flat – the venue for many such discussions – and hammered out the remaining difficulties. A 'brief and unremarkable' constitutional conference in Dar-es-Salaam paved the way for independence in December 1961. Nyerere complemented Macleod for his 'frankness and honesty and ... willingness to help'.[37] The Tanganyikan independence process was a model for what Macmillan hoped would happen: peaceful, orderly, yet rapid progression from colony status to independent Commonwealth member state. It also embodied a shift in priorities: readiness for independence was no longer to be measured by economic or social development; the ability to govern oneself effectively was now paramount. The Ugandan Conference held in September 1961 followed the same principles. The need to accommodate both local royalty and politicians made the task difficult, but by the end of the conference Macleod was able to announce that independence would take place in October 1962.

The matter of the Federation was to prove more troublesome and was the source of much friction between Macmillan, Macleod, Welensky and the Conservative Party. The issue of whether or not to release Banda marked the first clash between Macmillan and his Colonial Secretary.

Macleod saw Banda as the key to constitutional development in Nyasaland and favoured his immediate release in
order for him to meet the Monckton Commission during
its visit to the Federation. However, Commonwealth
Secretary Alec Douglas-Home was bitterly opposed, agree-
ing with Welensky that Banda's release should wait until
after the Commission had left. This split between the
Commonwealth Relations Office – responsible for the
Federation and Southern Rhodesia – and the Colonial
Office responsible for Nyasaland and Northern Rhodesia –
dogged Macmillan on the whole matter of the Federation.
Macmillan proposed to release Banda three days before
Monckton left Nyasaland, to which Macleod and Douglas-
Home agreed. While dismissed as a 'minor crisis' in
Macmillan's memoirs, the Banda disagreement had been a
major threat to Cabinet unity; Macleod had threatened to
resign over the matter.[38] Macmillan's intervention had pre-
vented a Party split, and was well rewarded: Banda was released on 1 April 1960 and broadcast an appeal for calm,
saying Macleod could be trusted. No security problems arose.

In October 1960, the Monckton Commission published
its findings. While officially recommending that the
Federation be maintained, the report nevertheless sounded
the death-knell for that unfortunate conglomerate. It recommended that the African franchise be extended, that
self-government in Northern Rhodesia should advance, and
that secession be discussed at the planned 1960 Federal
Constitutional review. The last two provisions incensed
Welensky, who urged Macmillan to reject the report.
Macmillan refused, and the constitutional review opened in
December of 1960. Weeks of discussion resulted in impasse
and the conference was closed *sine die.*

Despite the deadlock at the Federal level, the
Constitutional Conference for Northern Rhodesia went
ahead as planned in February of 1961. Both Macleod and
Macmillan recognised the need for Africans to take control
of their own political destiny. Macleod's aim was to bring
about parity between Europeans and Africans in the next territorial parliament, with African majority and independence

in the following one. Welensky opposed any such changes, and sought to mobilise British parliamentary sentiment against the proposals.

On 9 February, Macleod appeared before the Colonial Affairs Committee, where he was pressured into admitting that Her Majesty's Government still supported the idea of the Federation and the need to safeguard the rights of Europeans. An early day motion was proposed, which attracted over one hundred signatures. This was the making of a significant back-bench revolt; the motion was garnering support not only from the right wing of the party, but also from its centre. In the House of Lords, Lord Salisbury accused Macleod of being 'too clever by half'. On 21 February, Macleod fought back, aggressively defending the complex formula for roll voting. The challenge began to falter; some of the more centrist rebels drafted a separate motion, under the guidance of Rab Butler. By the end of February, only forty members still adhered to the original motion.

The collapse of the challenge provided Macleod with some respite, but by this stage his career had already been fatally wounded. The fracas in Parliament had been accompanied by Cabinet infighting between Macleod and new Commonwealth Secretary Duncan Sandys, with Macmillan often finding himself acting as a referee between his two ministers. Welensky had also proved exasperating, refusing all compromise proposals that gave Africans a majority in Northern Rhodesian legislative bodies. This imbroglio continued throughout the spring and summer, and Macmillan grew increasingly frustrated. On the one hand, he found himself having to placate the irascible Welensky, which took considerable charm and acumen. On the other hand, Macmillan also had to hold the Cabinet together by managing the acrimonious relationship between Macleod – 'a Highlander – which means that he is easily worked up into an emotional mood' – and Sandys – 'cool as a cucumber; methodical; very strong in character'.[39] In June a compromise was reached on the constitution, stopping short of an African majority. Yet the ordeal had taken a physical toll on

Macmillan: 'I have no more "elan vital"! I am finished!' Macmillan wrote after one particularly difficult Question Time.[40]

Someone had to give, and it was Macleod. The February back-bench challenge was the most serious since the election and the right wing, although chastened, had still a strident voice. Macmillan also tended to blame Cabinet turmoil on his Colonial Secretary.[41] In short, Macleod was seen as a political liability and a personal irritant. In October 1961 he was replaced by the Reginald Maudling, whose style Macmillan hoped would be less aggravating. In the end, Macmillan grew to regard Maudling as '*plus royaliste que le roi*', and Maudling himself admitted that he sought to continue down the path that Macleod had blazed.[42]

Macleod's contribution to Britain's disentanglement from Africa was considerable. He was liked, respected and trusted by African nationalist leaders, and was consequently able to gain their cooperation. In this manner, Britain managed to ally herself with the progressive forces sweeping the continent and sail with, rather than against, the winds of change. He was extremely shrewd, and he 'approached the problems of ... Africa rather as a good bridge player (which he was)'.[43] As for his dealings with the Conservative Party, Macleod attracted right-wing criticism and kept the pressure off Macmillan himself. He was also able to create a breach among hard-liners. He presented each decision as discrete and never admitted to any major change in the shape or speed of decolonisation policy.[44] Ultimately, Macleod increasingly became a liability in Parliament. This, coupled with his clashes with other cabinet members, sealed his fate.

Maudling's appointment certainly eased Cabinet tensions to a large degree, but in January 1962 conflict arose again. Sandys and Maudling threatened to resign over the pace of reform in Northern Rhodesia. Macmillan realised that once again the time had come to act. He foresaw 'hideous trouble' if Britain did not accept 'what now seemed the inevitable disintegration of the Federation', seeing force as the only possible means of maintaining the status quo.[45] In

March 1962, Macmillan ended the peculiar Colonial Office/Commonwealth Relations Office co-dominion over the Federation and appointed Rab Butler as Minister with responsibility for Central Africa. Maudling stayed on at the Colonial Office for another four months, during which time he engineered the Land Settlement Scheme that used £16.5 million of British money to resettle 70,000 African families on land purchased from European settlers. This removed the final hurdle to Kenya's independence in December 1963.

Welensky accused Butler of being an 'undertaker', a colourful if essentially accurate description of his role.[46] Events now moved rapidly towards the inevitable collapse of the Federation. Soon after Butler's appointment, the Cabinet approved African majority rule for Northern Rhodesia. By June, Butler was advising that Nyasaland was bound to secede and a constitutional conference was set up for November.[47] December saw the Cabinet agree to Nyasaland's request for secession, and in Southern Rhodesia, the newly elected Rhodesia Front Government chose to reject the Federation and concentrate on maintaining European paramountcy in its own territory. The Federation itself was declared defunct at the end of 1963. Nyasaland became the independent state of Malawi in July 1964 and Northern Rhodesia followed as the Republic of Zambia in October of the same year. Britain's tenure in Africa was almost at an end.

Macmillan's approach to African decolonisation was influenced by international considerations and events. The primary factor driving decolonisation in Africa was undoubtedly events within the territories themselves – particularly the threat of nationalist explosions. This is clear when one considers the catalytic effect of Hola and the Nyasaland riots of 1959. However, for Macmillan the international aspect of decolonisation was key; indeed, the primary goal of withdrawing from Africa was to maintain Britain's status as a great power. Three general areas of foreign policy considerations formed the international context of decolonisation: the experiences of other European colonial powers, the growth of the Afro-Arab-Asian group, and Britain's special relationship with the United States.

Britain was not the only imperial power facing hard choices during this period. France, Belgium and Portugal were also coming to grips with the winds of change and the way in which they handled them served as cautionary examples for Macmillan. Omnipresent in his mind was the risk of a bloody, draining colonial war, epitomised by the Algerian quagmire. To Welensky in 1962 Macmillan said: 'In Algeria the French have a million men under arms, and they have now suffered a humiliating defeat. It is too simple a reading of history to think that you can exercise control simply by the use of power.'[48] The Portuguese refusal to even consider relinquishing her hold on her African territories drew much criticism from the international community, and Macmillan held up British policy as progressive against this inflexible attitude. Further away in time and in space, but equally cautionary, were the French experience in Vietnam and the Dutch ordeal in Indonesia.

The débâcle in the former Belgian Congo was also a foreboding gust in the winds of change. Independence, granted in June 1960, was followed by a European exodus and United Nations involvement. Belgium was publicly pilloried for poorly preparing her colony for independence, as well as for her 'neo-imperialist' intervention. Macmillan saw the Belgians as caught in a somewhat tragic predicament, unsure of how to deal with the mess that they had left behind. There was some worry – particularly among the governors in East and Central Africa – that the chaos in the Congo could spread to British possessions, but the general Whitehall view of this danger was more sanguine, as British territories were seen as politically more developed than the former Belgian colony.[49] However, there was a direct link in the form of Roy Welensky's moral – and possibly material – support for Moise Tshombe, the secessionist leader of Katanga province.

French and Belgian colonial policy also served as a spur to British decolonisation. In 1958 President de Gaulle made a blanket offer to French colonies of autonomy within a French Community or independence. This move caused more concern in Whitehall as it increased pressure within British colonies for independence.[50] In addition, the French gambit meant that Britain now risked losing her lead in the march towards decolonisation. The stakes were raised in 1960, when Belgian announced that the Congo would receive independence at the end of June; it was feared that 'the speed of the Congolese transition into independence is bound to have reactions in British territories in Africa.'[51] Instead of being the first European power to withdraw from Africa, Britain was now in danger of being one of the last, ahead only of the brutal Portuguese.[52]

The process and result of decolonisation, so important to Macmillan, were threatened by these European moves. In an attempt to keep Britain's head above the currents of decolonisation, Macmillan (most likely prompted by Philip de Zulueta, his private secretary) raised the possibility of consultations with the French and Belgians regarding Africa. It was, he wrote, 'one of the few parts of the world in which the European powers still have direct influence.' On a larger scale, Macmillan also saw consultations as a means of countering Britain's increasing marginalisation in Europe: 'It may indeed be that co-operation in Africa might help to prevent the economic division of Europe.' These consultations did take place, mostly at the sub-ministerial level, but were little more than exchanges of information. Indeed, as Lennox-Boyd minuted, 'it was fifty years too late' to coordinate colonial policies.[53]

Macmillan was also keenly aware of another threat to British decolonisation policy, one presented by the growing size and importance of the so-called Non-Aligned bloc. The process of empire shedding that had reached Africa in the mid-late 1950s had already resulted in independence for most colonial possessions in Asia and the Middle East. These new states sought to stand apart from East–West aggression and strike out on their own neutralist foreign policy path. The worry was that these neutralists would unite under the banner of anti-colonialism and adopt an attitude hostile to the West, using the United Nations as a forum and tool for their campaign.[54] This sort of public pressure resulted in Britain being put on the defensive at the UN and forced them to justify constantly their handling of British colonial territories.

Macmillan did not approve of this meddling in British affairs. He saw UN involvement in British African territories as synonymous with admitting that the United Kingdom was incapable of managing the transition of its possessions from colonies to independent states. A policy of minimum cooperation was adopted, whereby Britain submitted information about her territories to the UN as a goodwill gesture in the hopes that this would appease the anti-colonialists. The 1960 General Assembly Declaration on the Granting of Independence to Colonial Countries and Peoples made it clear that neutralist pressure could not be put off forever. From then on British policy was to buy time in order 'to take the remaining colonial decisions as free as possible from United Nations pressure.'[55]

The Central African Federation posed the greatest risk of UN intervention in a British territory, and it was feared that the situation would 'go badly wrong ... [and] we must be ready for serious trouble from the Africans ... with India, the Arabs, and the Soviet Union each trying to make the most out of it.'[56] The scale of possible interference was not discussed, though it was tacitly assumed that it could range from the dispatch of fact-finding commissions to a Congo-style peacekeeping. In 1962 the United Nations Decolonisation Committee took up discussion of conditions in the Federation, prompting Macmillan to write in his diary: 'I see a new horror – the United Nations ... is to enquire into liberty in Southern Rhodesia!'[57] Despite this worry, the Federation was liquidated without any major UN involvement.

The United States also figured prominently in Macmillan's thinking about decolonisation. American foreign policy had been traditionally opposed to all forms of colonialism, and this attitude was a frequent sticking point in the Anglo-American special relationship.[58] Coupled with this anti-imperialist outlook was a tendency for the United States to view European influence in their colonial possessions as a stabilising factor in the context of containment. This resulted in a somewhat contradictory American approach to colonialism: while generally supportive of the liquidation of Europe's empires, the United States feared that the vacuum left behind would be filled by the Soviet Union. The 1950s were a time of particular ambivalence in American attitudes towards decolonisation, prompted mainly by the growing realisation of the need to accommodate nationalism in the developing world, but also by the desire to maintain good relations with the European powers. The trend that emerged was continued American pressure for the liquidation of colonial empires along with a growing willingness to become directly involved in former colonial territories.[59]

This placed Macmillan in a dilemma regarding his decolonisation policy and the special relationship. There was general distrust of the 'traditional unconstructive American attitude' towards decolonisation, which was seen as trying to push Britain to shed her Empire too quickly and without adequate preparation.[60] The motives of the United States were also seen as less than honourable. Philip de Zulueta minuted angrily in 1959 that 'the main American interest is to get a share in the exploitation of Africa's mineral resources.'[61] Macmillan did not share this mistrust, but he did agree that the 'persistent misperception by the Americans of our colonial policy is one of the most serious obstacles to a proper understanding between our two Governments.' He stressed the need to make the United States realise that the British path was the best available, and offered good prospects for creating a stable, pro-West Africa.[62]

As with the Europeans, Macmillan sought to strengthen Britain's position in the American circle through his decolonisation policy, primarily with bilateral consultations. These took place from 1959 onwards at the level of Assistant Under-Secretary (on the British side) and Assistant Secretary of State (on the American side). However, these consultations never went beyond explanation, and they seem to have had little effect on American policy. After a series of such meetings in November 1959, State Department officials told their British counterparts that the US 'believed that while the movement in the Federation might be generally in the right direction, the pace was altogether too slow.'[63] The subject of Africa was also frequently brought up at the ministerial level, with similar results.

The 1961 change of administration in the United States brought no improvement in Anglo-American understanding. If anything, President Kennedy was more determined that the Europeans should rid themselves of empire. In February, the visit of G. Mennen Williams, the new Assistant Secretary of State for African Affairs, caused some discomfort in Whitehall. There were fears that he would act like 'a bull in a china shop' but above all America was resented for not having sought British advice prior to the trip.[64] Even as late as April 1962, the Foreign Office was writing that it was 'absolutely essential for the peaceful evolution of Africa ... that we should not be harassed over the next year or two by constant pressure to go faster than we think wise.'[65]

To sum up, in setting the agenda for decolonisation, Macmillan had a profound and decisive effect. The question was never whether Britain should leave Africa. This issue had already been settled prior to Macmillan assuming the premiership. Macmillan's key contribution was to make Africa a priority and recognise the need to speed up the pace of decolonisation. In early 1959, a conference of East African governors agreed that the likely timetable for independence would be: Tanganyika in 1970, Kenya in 1975 and Uganda somewhere between the two.[66] As it transpired, independence was achieved for Tanganyika in 1961, Kenya in 1963 and Uganda in 1962; a fifteen-year timetable had been reduced by 80 per cent.

Macmillan also had a direct impact on the workings of colonial policy, primarily in his appointment of Iain Macleod. Macleod's hands-on approach, his deep commitment to decolonisation and his shrewdness were instrumental in advancing the cause of African representation, particularly in the Federation. Despite the Cabinet aggravation caused by Macleod's temperament and the troubles in Parliament, Macleod and Macmillan made a very good team. Together they managed to bypass then isolate both settler resistance in East and Central Africa and right-wing opposition in

Parliament. Welensky characterised Macleod as 'subtle and secretive', Macmillan 'as soothing as cream and as sharp as a razor'.[67] Eventually this teamwork was shipwrecked on the rocks of Cabinet squabbling and Parliamentary opposition, yet it did much to unpick the East and Central African knot.[68]

Domestic politics and foreign policy considerations beyond Africa influenced Macmillan's handling of decolonisation. The international context was of the utmost importance, Macmillan recognising both the cautionary examples of what could go wrong and the pressures for change that came from outside the British colonial sphere. Indeed, the ultimate goal of withdrawing from the Empire was to maintain Britain's status as a world power. Domestic political concerns played a role in determining the speed of decolonisation. Macmillan was first and foremost a politician, and he was careful not to risk fragmenting the Conservative Party over the colonial issue. This can be seen in his postponement of major initiatives in Africa until after the 1959 General Election and his reasons for dismissing Macleod.

Macmillan's success in managing the end of Empire in Africa can be evaluated on two levels. First, the withdrawal from Africa can be deemed a triumph for his policy. His rejection of force and recognition of the need to accommodate African nationalism resulted in an orderly departure without a traumatic colonial war. Seen in comparison with France's struggles in Indochina and Algeria, this is a major achievement. By the time he left office in October 1963, only Southern Rhodesia remained as a bastion of settler rule. Achieving majority rule there could only have been accomplished by military force, and Macmillan had no intention of going that route.[69] The Salisbury government remained Britain's only major African liability; there could have been many more. By and large Britain left behind independent states with a relatively high degree of political cohesion and institutionalisation, another success when compared to colonial powers such as Belgium and Portugal.[70]

On another level, Macmillan's success in maintaining Britain's global position was less complete. Through the process of decolonisation, he sought to maintain Britain's prestige. The speed with which Britain prepared her African territories was indeed impressive. However, the very fact that Britain was a colonial power stigmatised her, and there was little that Macmillan could do to change this perception. The ambiguous attitude of the Americans towards colonialism meant that they were difficult to please, while the Arab-Asian (and later African) states needed anti-imperialism as a cohesive force. No matter how fast Britain shed her Empire, she would still have been subject to criticism.

Macmillan's attempt to maintain Britain's great power status by strengthening the Commonwealth circle was similarly unsuccessful. [71] Yet it is clear that Macmillan regarded the Commonwealth as far more influential than it actually was. He saw it as a multiracial organisation, bound together by common bonds of freedom, morality and responsible government, and 'with an important role to play in the world struggle'.[72] His outlook was undoubtedly buoyed by the success of his 1958 tour of Commonwealth nations, which increased his stature as a statesman immeasurably.[73]

However, Macmillan placed too much faith in the Commonwealth's potential. It was not so much an organisation, but a gentleman's club which dealt in the currency of 'attitudes, values, intuitions, motivation'. From the point of view of decolonisation, this was significant inasmuch as it allowed former British colonies to come of age on the international scene with dignity, which was 'very much more important to the nationalist point than any concrete case about economic viability'.[74] Yet from the point of view of Britain's status as a great power, these intangibles did not translate the Commonwealth into a cohesive body. At the same time as its membership became multiracial and diverse, competing values and ideologies – such as Pan-Africanism and neutralism – were admitted. The centripetal attraction of the Commonwealth could not stand up to these centrifugal forces, as the difficult Prime Ministers' Conferences of 1960 and 1962 showed.

Although Macmillan sought to play the Commonwealth card in order to increase British influence in the European and American circles, his efforts did not prove fruitful. The

United States was frequently irritated at Britain's inability to influence what were seen as anti-Western policies of certain Commonwealth members such as India and Ghana.[75] In negotiations over the EEC, British attempts to maintain special trade preferences for Commonwealth goods only served to alienate the Europeans. In both cases, Britain's attempts to support the Commonwealth circle damaged her influence in the other two.

Macmillan's expectation that he could use the process and result of decolonisation to maintain Britain's status as a great power 'proved a forlorn hope'.[76] This reflects something of the nature of British power in the post-1945 international arena. Power is a relationship between states, based upon a series of tangibles – such as wealth, population, territory – and intangibles.[77] Among the latter are influence and prestige, the two quantities that Macmillan sought to augment through decolonisation. The tangible aspects of British power had been in decline since the beginning of the twentieth century and after the trauma of the Second World War they stood far below those of the United States and the Soviet Union. The process of shedding Empire was an attempt to swap dwindling tangible assets for increased intangibles, thereby maintaining British global power. In this respect, Macmillan failed. However, it must not be forgotten that were it not for his successful withdrawal from Africa, Britain's decline would have been considerably more traumatic.

NOTES

1.   D.A. Low (ed.), *Eclipse of Empire* (Cambridge: CUP, 1991), pp. 226–40.
2.   D.K. Fieldhouse, *Black Africa 1945–80: Economic Decolonisation and Arrested Development* (London: Allen & Unwin, 1986) pp. 6–7; R. Pearce, 'The Colonial Office and planned decolonisation in Africa', *African Affairs*, Vol. 83, No. 330 (January 1984), pp. 90–1.
3.   Memorandum by Commonwealth Relations Office (CRO) Parliamentary Under-Secretary Patrick Gordon Walker, 16 April 1951, quoted in R. Hyam, 'The geopolitical origins of the Central African Federation: Britain, Rhodesia and South Africa 1948–1953', *Historical Journal*, Vol. 30, No. 1 (1987), p. 155.

4. P. Gifford and W.R. Louis (eds), *The Transfer of Power in Africa: Decolonisation 1940–1960* (New Haven: Yale University Press, 1982), pp. 394–6; Lord Chandos, *The Memoirs of Lord Chandos* (London: Bodley Head, 1962), pp. 385–8.
5. Gifford and Louis, *The Transfer of Power in Africa*, pp. 414–15.
6. R. Welensky, *4000 Days: The Life and Death of the Federation of Rhodesia and Nyasaland* (London: Collins, 1964), p. 65.
7. Gifford and Louis, *The Transfer of Power in Africa*, p. 415.
8. Quoted in N. Fisher, *Harold Macmillan* (London: Weidenfeld & Nicolson, 1982), p. 82; A. Sampson, *Macmillan: A Study in Ambiguity* (London: Allen Lane The Penguin Press, 1967), pp. 58–9.
9. Quoted in D. Horowitz, 'Attitudes of British Conservatives towards decolonisation in Africa', *African Affairs*, Vol. 69, No. 274 (January 1970), p. 16.
10. D. Goldsworthy, 'Keeping change within bounds: aspects of colonial policy during the Churchill and Eden governments, 1951–57', *Journal of Contemporary History*, Vol. 18, p. 86; D.J. Morgan, *The Official History of Colonial Development*, Vol. V (London: Macmillan, 1980), p. 402.
11. R.F. Holland, *European Decolonisation 1918–1981: An Introductory Survey* (London: Macmillan, 1985), p. 204.
12. Low, *Eclipse of Empire*, pp. 167–8.
13. Low, *Eclipse of Empire*, pp. 209, 211–12; Horowitz, 'Attitudes of British Conservatives', p. 110.
14. W.R. Louis and H. Bull (eds), *The Special Relationship: Anglo-American Relations Since 1945* (Oxford: Clarendon, 1986), p. 277. W.R. Louis and R. Owen (eds), *Suez 1956: The Crisis and its Consequences* (Oxford: Clarendon, 1989), p. 185.
15. This fear was especially prevalent in the Colonial Office. See: PRO: CO 35/10638.
16. A. Sampson, *Anatomy of Britain* (London: Hodder & Stoughton, 1962), p. 340.
17. H. Macmillan, *Riding the Storm, 1956–1959* (London: Macmillan, 1971), p. 414.
18. Fisher, *Harold Macmillan*, p. 186.
19. Gifford and Louis, *The Transfer of Power in Africa*, p. 402.
20. On the role of Conservative politics in Macmillan's colonial policy, see D. Goldsworthy, *Colonial Issues in British Politics 1945–1961* (Oxford: Clarendon, 1971) and Horowitz, 'Attitudes of British Conservatives'.
21. Quoted in Sampson, *Macmillan*, p. 129.
22. Goldsworthy, *Colonial Issues in British Politics 1945–1959* (Oxford: Oxford University Press, 1971), p. 314. See also Sampson, *Macmillan*, pp. 131–2.
23. Africa: The Next Ten Years', 2 December 1959, PRO: FO 371/137972.
24. Macmillan to Lloyd, 2 July 1959, PRO: PREM 11/2587.

25. Lennox-Boyd to Macmillan, 30 July 1959, PRO: PREM 11/2587.
26. Lloyd to Macmillan, 28 July 1959, PRO: PREM 11/2587.
27. Low, *Eclipse of Empire*, p. 245.
28. Macmillan, *Riding the Storm*, pp. 746, 734.
29. Macmillan, *Riding the Storm*, p. 738.
30. A. Horne, *Macmillan 1957–1986* (London: Macmillan, 1989), p. 180.
31. Horne, *Macmillan 1957–1986*, pp. 182–3.
32. Horne, *Macmillan 1957–1986*, p. 185.
33. H. Macmillan, *Pointing the Way, 1959–61* (London: Macmillan, 1972), p. 156.
34. Horne, *Macmillan 1957–1986*, p. 195.
35. Quoted in N. Fisher, *Iain Macleod* (London: Deutsch, 1973), p. 142.
36. H. Macmillan, *At the End of the Day, 1961–1963* (London: Macmillan, 1973), p. 290.
37. Fisher, *Iain Macleod*, p. 153.
38. Horne, *Macmillan 1957–1986*, p. 202.
39. Horne, *Macmillan 1957–1986*, p. 407; Macmillan, *At the End of the Day*, p. 314.
40. Horne, *Macmillan 1957–1986*, p. 396.
41. Fisher, *Macmillan*, p. 245.
42. Macmillan, *At the End of the Day*, p. 318; R. Maudling, *Memoirs* (London: Sidgwick & Jackson, 1978), p. 99.
43. Sir Hilton Poynton, correspondence with the author, 11 June 1993.
44. Goldsworthy, *Colonial Issues*, p. 372; Horowitz, 'Attitudes of British Conservatives', pp. 25–6.
45. Horne, *Macmillan 1957–1986*, p. 408; Welensky, *4000 Days*, pp. 323–4.
46. Welensky, *4000 Days*, p. 329.
47. 'Nyasaland: Discussions with Dr. Banda in London', 20 June 1962, PRO: CAB 129/100 C.62.
48. Welensky, *4000 Days*, p. 323.
49. Note of meeting in the Secretary of State's room, 16 November 1959, PRO: CO 822/1451; Sir Evelyn Hone to W.B.L. Monson, 7 December 1959, PRO: CO 936/543p; telegram FO to Dakar, 1 February 1960, PRO: PREM 11/2883.
50. Horne, *Macmillan 1957–1986*, p. 177.
51. Congo Independence 7 July 1960, PRO: PREM 11/2883 JB1015/130.
52. Low, *Eclipse of Empire*, p. 246.
53. De Zulueta to Tim Bligh, 1 July 1959; Macmillan to Lloyd, 3 July 1959; Lennox-Boyd to Macmillan, 30 July 1959, all PRO: PREM 11/2587.
54. C. Bell, 'The United Nations and the West', *International Affairs*, Vol. 29, No. 4 (October 1953), pp. 466–8.
55. Macleod to Poynton, 10 August 1961, PRO: CO 936/681.
56. 'Afro-Asians at the 14th General Assembly', 19 January 1960, PRO: FO 371/153619.
57. Macmillan, *At the End of the Day*, p. 320.

58. See C. Fraser, 'Understanding American policy towards the decolonization of European empires', *Diplomacy and Statecraft*, Vol. 3, No. 1 (1992); D.C. Watt, *Succeeding John Bull: America in Britain's Place 1900–1975* (Cambridge: CUP, 1984).
59. See National Security Council Report NSC 5818, 26 August 1958, *FRUS, Vol. XIV Africa*, pp. 23–37.
60. Lennox-Boyd to Macmillan, 17 March 1957, PRO: PREM 11/3239.
61. De Zulueta to Tim Bligh, 1 July 1957, PRO: PREM 11/2587.
62. Lord Perth to Macmillan, 23 February 1957, PRO: PREM 11/2587.
63. 'Talks on Africa', 24 November 1959, PRO: FO 371/137972.
64. Caccia to Home, 10 March 1961; H.A.A. Hankey to de Zulueta, 27 February 1961; PRO: PREM 11/3600.
65. Brief on Washington Visit, 13 April 1962, PRO: PREM 11/3783.
66. Low, *Eclipse of Empire*, p. 246.
67. Welensky, *4000 Days*, pp. 187, 144.
68. Although management of Federation affairs was consolidated under Rab Butler in March 1962, Macmillan himself had recognised the problem of dual ministerial responsibility for the Federation as far back as May 1961 (Horne, *Macmillan 1957–1986*, p. 409).
69. Gifford, 'Misconceived Dominion: The Creation and Disintegration of Federation in British Central Africa', in Gifford and Louis (eds), *The Transfer of Power in Africa: Decolonisation 1940–1960* (New Haven: Yale University Press, 1982), p. 415.
70. W. Tordorff, *Government and Politics in Africa* (London: Macmillan, 1984), p. 38.
71. For a comprehensive assessment of the role of the Commonwealth in Macmillan's foreign policy see N. Mansergh, *The Commonwealth Experience: Volume Two* (London: Macmillan, 1982), pp. 173–89; Louis and Bull, *The Special Relationship*, pp. 365–78.
72. Macmillan, *Riding the Storm*, p. 414.
73. Horne, *Macmillan 1957–1986*, pp. 87–8.
74. Arnold Smith *First Secretary-General of the Commonwealth*, quoted in A.P. Thornton 'The Transformation of the Commonwealth and the "Special Relationship"', in Louis and Bull (eds) *The 'Special Relationship': Anglo-American Relations since 1945* (Oxford: Oxford University Press, 1985), p. 376; ibid., p. 367.
75. Louis and Bull, *The Special Relationship*, p. 255.
76. J.G.T. Tahourdin, correspondence with the author, 17 March 1993.
77. D. Reynolds, 'Power, wealth and war in the modern world', *Historical Journal*, Vol. 32, No. 2 (1989), p. 483.

6 Staying in the Game? Coming into the Game? Macmillan and European Integration
Sabine Lee

The European-mindedness of Britain, even more than two decades after the country's entry to the then EEC, has not ceased to attract popular and academic debate. Similarly, the European-mindedness of the United Kingdom's political leaders has been the cause of much controversy. Harold Macmillan, who steered British policy onto a more Europe-oriented course, is no exception to this. While he saw himself as a 'European' and while many agree that he did a great deal to promote ideas of European integration and British participation in it, others argue that the conduct of his policy at best did not serve British interests in the European context and at worst hampered them. Macmillan's Europeanism has been called into question, most recently by Richard Davenport-Hines, who stated, referring to de Gaulle's first veto of British entry into the EEC:

> Although the pretext for de Gaulle's veto seems dubious with hindsight, his instincts about Harold Macmillan were sound enough. The latter had always blown hot and cold over Europe and his commitment to 'interdependence' with the Americans had no limit; like the British people themselves, he would have been an ambivalent, perhaps even a retarding influence in European development.[1]

Between 1955, the year of the Messina initiative of the ECSC Six and 1963, the first rejection of British admission to the EEC by General de Gaulle, the British radically altered their policy on European cooperation and integration. Obviously, this did not happen in a political vacuum, merely due to a change of mind of the political leadership, but was the outcome of an agonising reappraisal involving policy-makers as well as the bureaucracy, the public as well as non-governmental élites. In order to throw light on the role which Harold Macmillan played in the process, two phases of partic-ular importance for the course of opinion formation on this issue will be looked at: the years 1955–56, when the British formed their initial response to the Messina initiative which was to lead to the foundation of the European Economic and Atomic Communities, and the years 1960–61, the period im-mediately preceding Macmillan's announcement that the United Kingdom would seek to enter these communities. Then the breakdown of the free trade area negotiations and the first accession negotiations will be discussed briefly in order to relate expectations to achievements.

On 26 November 1956 the British Chancellor of the Exchequer, Harold Macmillan, announced in the House of Commons that Her Majesty's Government would seek to negotiate a free trade area that 'would consist of the Customs union ... together with such other countries, including our-selves, as thought fit to join'.[2] This was a reaction to the process of economic integration which had taken place on the continent since 1955. In June 1955, France, the Federal Republic of Germany, Italy and the Benelux countries, de-parting from previous predominantly intergovernmental approaches (the ECE, WEU and OEEC), passed a resolu-tion (Messina Resolution) aiming at the establishment of a 'united Europe by the development of common institu-tions, the progressive fusion of national economies, the creation of a Common Market and the progressive harmon-isation of their social policies'.[3]

The British took part in the Inter-Governmental Committee set up to work out the details of the common market under the chairmanship of Belgian Foreign Minister Henri Spaak (Spaak Committee) during the following months (until November 1955), though with little enthusiasm. They emphasised their non-committal role by stressing that their nominee, Russell Bretherton (Under-Secretary at the Board of Trade and the United Kingdom's member of the OEEC's Steering Board for Trade), was appointed 'representative' but not 'delegate'.[4] Gladwyn Jebb, later one of the main advocates of European integration, believed that 'no very spectacular developments' could be expected as the result of Messina,[5] and Treasury and Board of Trade studies continued to believe that it would be undesirable to become too closely involved in the integration process. Although declining Commonwealth trade was recognised as a factor which made an industrial trade arrangement with the Six advisable, participating in a common market was out of the question.[6]

It is only consistent with the general scepticism about the prospect of European integration that both Eden as Prime Minister and Macmillan as Foreign Secretary did not take an active part in the formulation of European policy in the latter half of 1955. There seemed to be little reason to 'worry' about the success of the Six, and this alleged lack of urgency explains why the running of European business was left to officials in the Foreign Office, Treasury and Board of Trade, while the governmental foreign policy élite dealt with seemingly more important matters. When Macmillan, for instance, was invited to attend the ministerial meeting discussing the interim report of the Spaak Committee in September 1955 the Foreign Office seemed far from sorry that the Foreign Secretary was engaged in discussions on Cyprus, and it was made clear that the British did not want ministerial association of any kind with the project of the Six at that stage.[7]

In the Spaak Committee, the British insisted on the need to avoid overlap with or duplication of the work of the OEEC, the organisation through which the United Kingdom hoped to reach further European integration on an intergovernmental level. The discussions also showed fundamental differences in the respective approaches to

European cooperation of the Messina Six, which were aiming at a customs union, and Britain, which favoured the concept of a free trade area.

In the end these distinct opinions led to British withdrawal from the work of the Spaak Committee. As the success of the Inter-Governmental Committee was much in doubt in 1955 – even in late 1955 – not only in the view of the British but also in the opinion of most other non-Messina countries, few people realised that the British withdrawal in November 1955 would be a 'critical turning point in the relations between the Six and the United Kingdom and the beginning of a long period of tension between the two'.[8]

If Great Britain and other non-Messina countries had not expected quick success of the Six, the tables were certainly turned at the Foreign Ministers' Conference in Venice in May 1956 at which the Six could account remarkable progress on the way to establishing a Common Market. Faced with the intergration endevours of the Six, the Mutual Aid Commitee (MAC) had established a working group to study the effects of a potential common market. The findings of this group under the chairmanship of Burke Trend, Permanent Under-Secretary in the Treasury, suggested that if a common market were to materialise, Britain might be forced to associate herself with it.[9] This directed the MAC to study an alternative trade arrangement which eventually led to 'Plan G', a proposal for an industrial free trade area.[10] Hence, on 19 July 1956, the Secretary-General proposed, and the Council of Ministers of the OEEC adopted, what was generally assumed to be a British initiative: the establishment of a working party to study the 'possible forms and methods of association, on a multilateral basis, between the proposed Customs Union and Member countries not taking part therein'[11] – in other words a free trade area.

In the months between the OEEC resolution to set up this working party and its first meeting on 25 September 1956, the British government for the first time attempted to work out a negotiating position for the free trade area discussions, and in August the issue was on the Cabinet agenda for the first time.[12] Although there was still a great deal of

scepticism regarding the future success of the Six, the determination to develop a negotiating concept for the United
Kingdom grew.

In the first full-length debate in the House of Commons,
on 26 November 1956, Harold Macmillan, announced the
result of the intragovernmental decision-making process,
namely that the British government would suggest the establishment of a 'mutual free trade area with the Messina
Powers and all other OEEC countries'.[13] This declaration
was supported by both Houses as well as by influential interest groups in the country.[14]

Which considerations affected this decision? To what
extent was it Harold Macmillan's own making, i.e. what was
his role in setting the European agenda? Why did the
British in 1955 stop short of full participation in the process
of integration just as they had done in the preceding
decade and would do again the years until 1961?

The British position towards the European integration
process differed substantially from the continental approach due to the distinct role Britain had played as an imperial and colonial power. British aspirations were to a great
extent extra-European. Winston Churchill's theory of
Britain being at the centre of three interlined circles – the
Commonwealth, the Anglo-American Alliance and Europe
– still dominated foreign policy thinking in the United
Kingdom, and during the immediate postwar years the UK
was still leaning heavily towards the United States and the
Commonwealth.

After the upheavals in the international setting since
1945, one might have expected a reappraisal of these underlying principles, but this appears not to have taken
place. When the United Kingdom started showing greater
interest in continental Europe after the Conference of
Venice in May 1956, it maintained many of its old tenets. An
indication of the fact that the British decision to turn to the
continent was not an immediate reaction to the integration
process or even a desire to participate in this process is
found in the 'timing' of the change of European policy.
Britain's attitude towards European integration did not

undergo any noticeable change until the middle of 1956. That is to say that the Conference of Messina, which was a crucial step on the way towards economic and eventually political union among the Six, was not the decisive momentum for Britain to turn away from her traditional European policy. Moreover, although parts of Whitehall started to recognise the economic significance of developments of European integration among the Six, it was not until the early 1960s that the British government as a whole began seriously to reconsider the basic principles of her European policies rather than the medium-term tactics.

The proposals for the free trade area, the British alternative to the movement towards European integration, were developed from essentially unchanged premises of previous European policies. Whilst before, British conceptions in regard to Europe had appeared feasible, this was no longer so because many conditions had changed. A clear example of this is the role which Commonwealth considerations played in the decision-making process on European integration issues.

The Commonwealth had substantially altered its structure. For instance, Great Britain was no longer the main importer of goods from the Commonwealth, and she was losing her pre-eminence as a trading partner for many Commonwealth countries.[15] Conversely the significance of the Commonwealth as a trading partner for Great Britain had increased.[16] In 1956 the still significant proportion of 49 per cent of British imports and 45 per cent of British exports remained within the Commonwealth, but a Commonwealth Relations Office analysis of the trends of traditional trade relations indicated that the Commonwealth would eventually lose its outstanding impact on British economy to Europe, and indeed this was the case in later years. Given the categorical British opinions on issues such as agriculture or the exclusion of overseas territories or even the association of developing OEEC countries, all of which were defended by pointing at Commonwealth responsibilities, it seems that the structural change which was in progress in the Commonwealth, namely the centripetal disintegration, was not taken into account when formulating the British negotiating position in the free trade area discussions.

British inability to reform is well characterised by William Wallace: 'Typically, a body of wise men is asked to consider some aspects of the problem, not including the underlying assumptions and objectives, and produces a report; which is then either implemented in a fashion less coherent than the report had recommended or largely disregarded in the heat of the debate.'[17] Indeed, in 1956 a report from the Commonwealth Relations Office (CRO) accurately predicted the trends in the future developments in economic and political relations between the United Kingdom and the Commonwealth. But it concluded:

> ... the Commonwealth can hardly remain in being without the uniting bond of the United Kingdom and the monarchy ... Were the United Kingdom to stand by herself, her importance would still be great but immensely less than it is while she remains the centre of the Commonwealth. If that is so, it will be vital in decisions to give the fullest weight to the necessity to keep the Commonwealth together, and to the Commonwealth reactions.[18]

Britain saw the famous three circles as a zero-sum game. Winning in the European circle necessarily meant losing in the other two circles. Thus, given the importance attached to the Commonwealth and the US links, activity on the European front was not an option.

In other words, despite the centripetal forces that caused the Commonwealth to disintegrate, and turned it into a highly questionable concept, it was to be preserved as an end in itself. This policy was not completely uncontested, as Treasury comments suggest,[19] but the main policy in the years of the free trade area negotiations was that indicated in the CRO report. It was not until 1959–60 that a significant number of officials and politicians opened their eyes to the fact that advancement in one of the three circles did not preclude success in the others. Only then did the Commonwealth links begin to be seen in a different light by more than just a handful of officials.

The emphasis on Commonwealth relations was just one indication of the British inability to recognise the signs of future developments. Just as Britain in 1951–52 had failed to realise the impact of the European Coal and Steel Community had on the process of European integration, a failure which made the Foreign Secretary Selwyn Lloyd admit in 1960 that he believed the British had 'made a mistake in not taking part in the negotiations which led to the formation of the Coal and Steel Community',[20] the government in 1955 clearly failed to understand the significance of the Messina initiative. As Bretherton put it: 'I don't think the Cabinet took much notice of it [the Messina Resolution] at the time,[21] which was judged to be 'merely another elaborate paper scheme of the continentals, and nearly certain to fail'.[22]

So the United Kingdom stood aside because no strategic decision was taken at the time of the Messina Conference in 1955. Britain's turn to Europe after the Conference of Venice in May 1956 was not brought about by the realisation that changing conditions in international relations meant that the basic principles underlying her foreign policy were no longer valid. Otherwise these tenets would have been modified to fit the situation of the 1950s. On the contrary, European policy in the late 1950s was an attempt to fit the old maxims of foreign policy into the new developments on the continent and elsewhere in the world. Although in retrospect this 'adjustment' appears half-hearted, the nature of this move was unprecedented in the sense that it was realised that relations with continental Europe began to play a more important role in British foreign policy considerations. 'Europe began to move up the scale, the Commonwealth to move down, and the nature of the British relations with the United States began to come into better perspective.[23]

The turn towards Western Europe coincided with the Suez Crisis, the experience of which had two effects of particular importance in the European context. On the continent it left the feeling that the United States dominated the Western response to the crisis, and the Europeans did not want to accept their dependence on the 'big' ally any longer. Also, the imminent danger of a Russo-American rapprochement without a European say promoted efforts to develop Europe into a 'third force'.

Naturally considerations about a future Europe that could fulfil such a task gave impetus to the integration process of the Six. Most politicians agreed that the weakness on the European side, exhibited in the Suez disaster, was a result of discord among the Western European countries, and hence it was assumed that speaking with one voice would strengthen Western Europe as a political force.

The emphasis on the necessity to overcome discord in Europe produced a first effect in the reaction to the military intervention in Suez. Despite the fact that none of the European states approved of the methods of the intervention, Germany, Italy and many other European countries (or more precisely European governments) tolerated this use of force for the sake of European unity instead of adding to the destabilisation of the United Kingdom and France by open criticism.

Leaving aside the 'real' political implications of the Suez Crisis, the embarrassing disfavour and opposition of the Americans caused temporary disillusionment in Britain with the transatlantic special relationship.[24] This 'psychological' factor was intensified by the realisation that the former world power Britain had declined, so that like other European states she would find it increasingly difficult to protect her national interests independently. Moreover, the British decline coincided with the relative rise of continental European strength, and the United Kingdom had to come to terms with the effects that a stronger continental European unity would have on her economic and political situation.

The perception of the weakening relations with the Commonwealth and the experiences of Suez were important elements in the decision to turn to continental Europe, for they made Britain realise that she 'could not afford to stay out'. This 'negative' argument dominated the debate for a long time, particularly over the economic aspects of the free trade area negotiations. It was not the 'positive' new foreign political approach that made the British take a fresh unprejudiced approach to European integration.

It was no coincidence that the 'Europeans' within the British political élite (Macmillan, Maxwell Fyfe, Thorneycroft, Eccles and Sandys) had come to a more realistic view of the Commonwealth and that they questioned the idealised picture painted by those who preached isolationism from continental Europe. Most of the new, mostly younger, guard did not share the belief in a British superpower status, and they argued that the only way to match the United States and the Soviet Union while at the same time containing Germany was within the framework of a united Europe.

This view was certainly held by Harold Macmillan whose fight for European ideals just as his enthusiasm for East–West *détente*, summitry and disarmament can be traced back to his wartime experience, most notably his experiences during the First World War when he lost many close friends in the trenches. Already in 1939, Macmillan was writing:

> Many people are asking what kind of Europe one could expect to emerge out of the chaos of today. The picture can only be painted in the broadest colours. But if the western civilisation it to survive, we must look forward to an organisation, economic, cultural, and perhaps even political, comprising all the countries of western Europe.[25]

This attitude was underlying Macmillan's engagement in the European Movement in which he took an active part in the early postwar years, and it also influenced his speech at the first assembly of the Council of Europe in September 1949 when he argued for an admission of the Federal Republic of Germany to the Council.[26]

Although the need to contain Germany in the postwar world order was perceived as important, the overriding consideration of the British desire to unite Europe was the ambition to stabilise the divided Europe and to counter the Soviet threat. Without unity, understood less politically than culturally, Britain feared Europe would not be capable of facing Soviet expansionism. But even if this cultural unity were to be achieved, the British insisted, it was only with American power and military assistance that the communists could be kept in check while at the same time binding the potentially disruptive Germans to Western Europe.

Hence, Macmillan's Europeanism, as with most British 'pro-Europeans', was not equivalent to that of continental European federalists like Spaak, Monnet, Adenauer or de Gasperi. The British envisaged a much wider geographical framework; they allowed for – in fact demanded – a definite place for the United States in the system. They were looking for a confederation rather than a federation, and, most importantly, within the 'Euro-Atlantic' system they attributed the prominent link of the chain between Europe and the United States to the United Kingdom. Consequently, although the pro-Europeans tried to fight the notion coined by Roger Makins and adopted among others by Winston Churchill that Britain was 'of but not in Europe', they were by no means committed to federalism or integration. All the 'European' proposals from the Macmillan-Eccles resolution of September 1950, outlining a modified Coal and Steel Community which would allow British participation,[27] down to the free trade Association were in line with this approach.[28]

Even with this wider European concept which did not encompass the much-dreaded surrender of national sovereignty or political union, the pro-Europeans did not prevail in 1955–56, the phase which proved decisive for whether Britain would stay in or out. The reasons for this are manifold, but among the most important factors are the decision-making process and the interplay between economic and political arguments.

In the years immediately after the Messina initiative the Treasury and the Board of Trade dominated the formulation of policy on European cooperation. Not only were the Mutual Aid Committee and the Economic Steering Committee chaired by Treasury officials, but Treasury officials by far outnumbered those of other departments at all the MAC meetings.[29] Another indication of the lack of involvement of foreign secretaries was that unlike most Cabinet Committees with Foreign Office representation

(Defence, Africa, Security, Colonial Policy), where the Foreign Secretary represented the Office, in the Committee for European Economic Association, the Lord Privy Seal was formally a member and the Foreign Secretary was not.[30]

Therefore the reductionist view on Europe, the belief that the issue should be treated mainly as an economic and not a political affair, was enhanced by the fact that European policies fell under the responsibility of the Treasury and Board of Trade and not the Foreign Office. It is difficult to distinguish between cause and effect in this context. But it appears that the Foreign Office's lack of interest fed back into the issue being considered predominantly in economic terms, and conversely, the economic approach ensured that the Foreign Office shunned responsibility for European policies. In any case, it is hardly surprising that the proposals for the free trade area were made by the Chancellor of the Exchequer, Harold Macmillan, and the President of the Board of Trade, Peter Thorneycroft, and that the Foreign Secretary was not closely involved in the discussions. In fact Eden and Lloyd were not, on the whole, convinced about the concept. Antony Eden was 'not interested in the economic side of Europe'[31] and Selwyn Lloyd certainly did not make headlines as a pressing Europeanist immediately after his appointment as Foreign Secretary either.

British reaction to Messina and the situation in which Russell Bretherton found himself as the British representative in the Spaak Committee was symptomatic of the British position towards Europe in 1955. The formal reply to the invitation to participate as a full and equal partner in the negotiations following the Messina Conference was sent by Harold Macmillan, then Foreign Scretary. His Dutch counterpart, Jacques Beyen, had discussed the issue with both Macmillan and the less enthusiastic Chancellor of the Exchequer, Rab Butler, and Beyen left London with the impression that at least Macmillan had been won over to the idea of Britain joining the integration process of the Six.[32] However, Macmillan's reply was negative, emphasising the British difficulties with any project of a European Common Market based on a common external tariff. Therefore, any participation of the United Kingdom had to be without commitment. As Macmillan phrased it in his memoirs: 'It was our wish to take an active role in the work of the committee, but of course, without prior commitment to the resolution which was shared by the other countries.[33] It is worth noting that in Cabinet Macmillan had taken a rather different line advocating a more committed British role:

> [Macmillan] said that while we should preserve our full freedom of action to make it clear that we were in no way committed to joining any body or bodies which might eventually be set up, we might be able to exercise greater influence in the forthcoming discussions if we were to enter them *on the same footing* as the other countries concerned [my emphasis] and not in the capacity of observers.[34]

This suggests that the then Foreign Secretary Macmillan might have been prepared to go much further than other Cabinet members, but he had to bow to the pressures of less European-minded forces such as Eden and Butler. Butler, Chairman of the OEEC at the time, called the Messina meetings 'archaeological excavations', and he later stated that he and the Prime Minister (Eden) were simply 'bored' with the European question.[35]

The policy of 'no commitment' left Bretherton with little or no room for manoeuvre, and, in fact, it reflected the governmental attitude that moves of any kind were undesirable, because they demanded attention and ultimately decisions which the government was not prepared to take.

Bretherton reported back to London urging the government to take action:

> If we are prepared to take a firm line, that we want to come in, and will be part of this, we can make this body into whatever we like. But if we don't say that, something will probably happen and we shan't exercise any influence over it ... we have the power to guide the conclusion of this conference in almost any direction we like, but beyond a certain point we cannot exercise the power without becoming responsible for the results.[36]

But, as Bretherton perceived it, again nobody took any notice.

Since the British free trade area proposals were a reaction to the continental European integration process, British attitudes in the course of the negotiations depended on the evaluation of this process by certain officials at a particular time. When Macmillan proposed a free trade area in November 1956, it was still not entirely clear where the discussions of the Messina powers would lead.[37] By the time the OEEC Council of Ministers adopted the resolution to enter negotiations in February 1957 this had changed,[38] and six weeks later the Rome Treaties were signed. By this time, however, the British had long crossed the point beyond which they could no longer influence the inner dynamism of continental integration.

When it was announced in the House of Commons on 31 July 1961 that Britain would seek entry to the EEC, again it was Harold Macmillan who broke the news about a change of direction in European policy. If the decision to negotiate a free trade area with the Messina Six OEEC partners in 1956 had indicated that British governmental views towards European integration and British participation were shifting, the decision to join the EEC was a U-turn taken after an even more agonising and more controversial reappraisal by Cabinet, parliamentarians and public.

The reasons for the drastic change of direction have been the subject of much debate, and with archival sources on the accession negotiations now available argument has intensified. After a short reminder of the changes that had occurred in the late 1950s, particular attention will be paid here to the role the Prime Minister played in this reappraisal.

The signing of the Treaties of Rome had led to increasing cohesion between the Six. Attempts at bridge-building between the EEC Six and the other OEEC member countries proved unsuccessful and only resulted in the creation of the rival economic bloc, the European Free Trade

Association (EFTA). The failure of the British effort to re-
strain the Six from furthering their unification process by
forming a wider or even rival economic grouping was only
one indication of declining British influence in international affairs. This decline in power and status became increasingly obvious in the late 1950s and in particular in 1960
and 1961. It had severe repercussions for Macmillan's personal standing. The British Prime Minister, at a time of lack
of US leadership due to Dulles' illness, had taken the lead in
the sphere of East–West relations with his visit to Moscow in
February/March 1959. This had been rewarded by a stunning electoral success, but in terms of international relations
Macmillan's action had been less of an achievement. The
collapse of the 1960 summit brought home to Macmillan the
limits of his own personal influence and also those of British
impact on international relations. Britain could no longer
compete as one of the great powers, a fact obvious since at
least the Suez débâcle and reinforced by the abandonment
of Blue Streak, Britain's independent nuclear deterrent. The
Prime Minister tried to mediate when the shooting down of
the American U2 plane over the Soviet Union jeopardised
the impending high-level talks in which he wanted to bring
the Cold War to an end. The futility of this endeavour
demonstrated to Macmillan that his role as mediator
between the USA and USSR had been short-lived. The
significance of this aspect in the Prime Minister's reviving interest in European affairs was highlighted by his Private
Secretary, Philip de Zulueta, who claimed that 'the failure of
the 1960 summit was really crucial in the development of his
concept in Europe because at the summit it became apparent that he really couldn't by himself bring irreconcilable
American and Russian positions closer.'[39]

It would be an oversimplification to attribute Macmillan's
return to the issue of European integration to the mere
desire to go down in history as one of the great statesmen
bringing political or economic peace, but without doubt the
lack of success in furthering *détente* and the wish to stay on
the international stage as one of the main actors were contributing factors in his reorientation.

Furthermore, the time was ripe for a change in European policy not least because of changing economic conditions. It has already been pointed out that the Commonwealth had undergone substantial structural changes in the 1950s. The results of this and the effect upon the cohesion of the Commonwealth were even more obvious in 1960 than during the first phase of British reappraisal of her position towards continental Europe in 1955–56. This, coupled with the economic success of the Common Market and the relatively weak performance of the United Kingdom, forced the British government, the Conservative Party and the Prime Minister himself to reconsider the British position.

Harold Macmillan was doubtless influential in bringing about the change in the British European outlook. The first step in this direction was within the wider foreign policy context when Macmillan set up the Future Policy Study. It was established in June 1959 in order to comment on the main political, economic and military developments until 1970 and possible British reactions. Apart from the Prime Minister himself the highest officials from the Foreign Office (Hoyer Millar), Treasury (Makins) and Ministry of Defence (Powell) were among the initiators,[40] and this indicates the intended broad scope of the study. As one of the main areas of concern emerged the process of European cooperation, and it appears that this result of the Future Policy Study had considerable impact on the Prime Minister.

Looking at the year preceding the British decision to join the Common Market, one gets the impression of the Prime Minister and his political friends working busily, but in an almost clandestine way, to create a pro-European atmosphere, and using that to prepare the ground for the eventual U-turn in European policy. After the breakdown of the free trade area negotiations in 1958, Europe had been almost a non-issue. This changed at the end of 1959, in the aftermath of the general elections. As Beloff put it, Macmillan and his confidants 'began thinking that it would be to the party's advantage to shift public attention before the next elections towards a fresher and more progressive cause of union with Europe.'[41] The first major visible step in this direction was the Cabinet reshuffle at the end of July 1960 which placed pro-Europeans in strategically important positions: Christopher Soames became Minister of Agriculture, Fisheries and Food, and Duncan Sandys took over the Ministry of Commonwealth Relations, while Edward Heath moved to become Lord Privy Seal and in this position was to become Britain's most important negotiator of European affairs. The most subtle move, however, in this round of appointments was that of Rab Butler to the ministerial subcommittee dealing with the opening of the negotiations with the EEC Six known as HOPS. This neutralised one of the most powerful Eurosceptics in the Macmillan Cabinet.

Throughout the year 1960 the Foreign Office, Board of Trade and Treasury had been labouring over the pros and cons of closer links with the Common Market. Following the conclusion of the Future Policy Study, the Economic Steering Committee for Europe (ESE) had been established. The purpose of this committee, first under the chairmanship of Makins and from January 1960 on under Sir Frank Lee, was to study the long-term policy on European cooperation. General thoughts were directed into a more concrete investigation when the Prime Minister concluded at a meeting of the European Economic Association Committee in May 1960 that 'consideration ought to be given to joining the EEC as a full member' and 'that officials should be asked to answer certain questions (circulated by the Prime Minister) to assist the Ministers to reach a decision'.[42]

In reply to Macmillan's request, the ESE recommended that 'near-identification with the Common Market is the right object to pursue'.[43] The Foreign Office compiled a paper which summarised departmental opinions. Although 'in the Foreign Office view, which [was] shared by most Departments there [were] strong reasons of foreign policy for joining the European Economic Community as a full member' it emerged from the papers that some of the economic and commercial consequences were seen to 'rule out the possibility of simple adhesion to the Treaty of Rome'.

However, the paper concluded that the long-term British objective had to be to join the EEC.[44] Even more revealing than the policy paper which repeated the well-known economic and political arguments for and against joining (Commonwealth obligations, trade patterns, economic competitiveness, political cohesion, sovereignty, etc.) was the Permanent Under-Secretary's reaction to the paper. Frederick Hoyer Millar commented: 'I must confess that, as far as I myself am concerned, although I agree that the political arguments in favour of joining the community are strong, all my instinct are against doing so. Although one's mind thinks one ought to join, one's heart is against it.' This sums up the feelings of many at the time. Their hearts were against it, and this made the issue a particularly touchy one!

The Prime Minister recognised this, but he continued to work for a change of mind and heart. Having convinced himself of the inevitability (and virtue) of closer associations with the EEC, Macmillan was the crucial figure in directing other more hesitant forces in Britain towards the same conclusion. And now, in 1960, as head of government he no longer had to succumb to Cabinet and prime ministerial decisions as he had had to in 1955 and 1956 as Foreign Secretary and Chancellor of the Exchequer. Even though Macmillan 'did not establish a political crusade of the matter',[45] he regarded the issue as one of utmost importance – yet one of great sensitivity. Therefore he chose what he regarded as the most promising tactics to exploit to the full his prime ministerial powers while at the same time minimising the influence of potentially critical voices. The above-mentioned Cabinet reshuffle was only one example of this.

Another example was the way in which Macmillan controlled the Cabinet. By the end of 1960 Macmillan had finally made up his mind on the European bid, and he started working towards its realisation in a more determined manner. Little by little he tried to win support from other European leaders, but even more importantly from his Cabinet colleagues. The methods Macmillan used bore some resemblance to the situation in early 1959 when he circumvented the Cabinet by announcing his Moscow visit without consulting his colleagues and thereby ensured that he could follow his policy of high-level talks and summitry against potential Cabinet disagreement. In 1960–61, the Prime Minister again controlled the Cabinet agenda, this time by delaying discussions about the issue until he was certain to have secured the support of a majority of his Cabinet colleagues.[46] It is not strictly speaking true as Nora Beloff claims that 'there was no historic Cabinet meeting at which the decision was solemnly and formally taken: ministers discovered their leader's intentions gradually, at different times.'[47] The Cabinet unanimously decided in principle that the Prime Minister should announce that the British government would apply to enter the Common Market.[48] Nevertheless, the spirit of Beloff's assessment is correct. The decision was not taken after controversial Cabinet discussions, but after slow and enduring exertion of prime ministerial influence.

Macmillan also proved to be a master of timing with his actual announcement of the Cabinet decision in Parliament. Nora Beloff vividly describes the situation:

> The Prime Minister had carefully arranged to announce his decision on the last day of July as everybody was leaving London for the August Bank Holiday – the moment least conducive to the organization of conspiracies. The preparatory work on the various ranks of the Party, the Cabinet, the 1922 Committee, the key advisers at the Central Office had been faultless. Few other politicians in British history could have executed such a feat: Macmillan was about to go back on much of what he had said and done in ten years of office, including five years in Downing Street, without losing the smallest Parliamentary Secretary or Junior Whip along the way.[49]

From what has been outlined above three points have become clear. First, the fundamental decisions in the area of European cooperation and integration were influenced greatly by Macmillan both in their substance and in the way they were approached. Secondly, the Prime Minister was guided in his moves not only by the issue, but by foreign and domestic considerations. This is clear from the timing of both European initiatives which were reactions to European and world political events at the time and not merely European economic decisions. Thirdly, both phases of re-appraisal of British European policy were measures of crisis management. The proposal of a free trade area was a reac-tion to the success of the Messina Six which was threatening Britain economically and the United Kingdom reasoned that it 'could not afford to stay out'; the decision for a reorienta-tion of European policy towards integration with the conti-nent was reached during a time of crisis surrounding the decline of British political influence. Macmillan tried to join the European game in order to stay in the world power game.

Was Macmillan a Europeanist? He had a European vision as part of his vision of a worldwide 'peaceful coexistence'. But it would be going too far to argue that Macmillan had a European, let alone a federal European, programme. What distinguished him from most other political forces in Britain was his *interest* in Europe. He came to recognise that the three circles were not a matter of either/or, and that the reconciliation of the three areas had to take into account future developments as well as links and traditions of the past. Macmillan – unlike many other politicians – was prepared to fight the European battle when he thought the time was right, just as he fought the battles of *détente*, sum-mitry or the test ban treaty.

How successful was Harold Macmillan in what has been described as crisis management? Winning over domestic op-ponents is only half the battle – at the end of the day it was the negotiations with the European partners that decided on the success or failure of Macmillan's European policy, and from this point of view Macmillan's score looks far less impressive. The free trade area negotiations broke down in November 1958, and General de Gaulle vetoed British entry to the Community in January 1963, both with acquiescence of the other five EEC countries. Why did the British Prime Minister, who apparently succeeded in winning round his own people, fail to negotiate acceptable terms for cooperation with the EEC Six in these two important instances?

British European policy in the 1950s was largely reactive, trying to make the best of situations presented by moves of the continental Europeans. Therefore, the initiative was not in the hands of Britain, and, as pointed out above, the policy had the character of crisis management, and was perceived as such from the outside. Hence British concepts lacked credibility, and they were viewed with some sense of suspicion by the EEC Six.

More importantly, the British made some grave errors of judgement. They failed to acknowledge the increasing dynamism of the integration process in the mid-1950s and the resulting growing sense of cohesion among the Six. also, Britain failed to understand the determination of the European federalists and the threat that the Six 'would go it alone' was not taken seriously. Moreover, the British, and not least Macmillan himself, overestimated the British negotiating strength and the Prime Minister's impact on other European leaders, in particular the influence on Adenauer and de Gaulle. Macmillan assumed that the Germans, including the Chancellor, would be happy to support the free trade area and later the British accession to the EEC, and he counted on the Chancellor's help to balance the less favourable attitude of the French General. This was not entirely unreasonable. In fact, much of what Adenauer said in late 1958 and in 1962 could be interpreted to support this assessment. Looking at the events in hindsight easily leads to the false impression that the path of European integration was almost inevitable, that British policy was untimely and that Macmillan's misjudgement of what was obviously a strong Franco-German anti-British front in November 1958 and in January 1963 is close to incomprehensibility. Yet, it has to be borne in mind that the situation in the late 1950s and early 1960s was very much in flux. Neither the original success of the Messina Six in establishing a customs union nor the failure to negotiate a free trade area nor, indeed, de Gaulle's first veto to British accession were easily predictable from the start. A number of external factors, factors outside the immediate framework of European integration but also outside the direct influence of the British, came into play, particularly in the case of the breakdown of the free trade area negotiations. De Gaulle's return to power in the summer of 1958, his unexpectedly good relationship with the German Chancellor in conjuncture with the flaring up of a new Berlin Crisis was a poisonous mixture as far as the British free trade area proposals were concerned. With the threat hanging over Berlin, Adenauer decided that he could not put at risk the newly established friendship with the French President, and he acquiesced in the latter's dismissal of the free trade area plans. The subsequent ill-timed visit of the British Prime Minister to Moscow further eroded the previously good working relationship with the ageing Chancellor, and the atmosphere of satisfactory trust was replaced by one of mistrust on both parts, a factor which proved to be crucial in the development of foreign policy in the subsequent years.

If the collapse of the free trade area negotiations can be attributed, at least partly, to external determinants, the failure of the first succession negotiations was more clearly the result of the fact that the British had not learnt their diplomatic lessons from the mistakes of the 1950s. Macmillan still believed that he could negotiate with the Six on British terms, exerting influence on both Germany and France. Hence he continued to overestimate British bargaining powers. With the UK's economic position having declined relative to that of the Six and with de Gaulle having consolidated his domestic position, this reflected reality even less than in the late 1950s. So, it is perhaps not surprising that de Gaulle countered the rebuff caused by the Nassau Agreements between the Americans and the British by a show of strength. Being sure of Adenauer's principal support the General took a calculated risk to upset the EEC. He was right in figuring that the Six were not prepared to exchange the well-established and successful Community with British participation at the risk of French withdrawal.

It has been argued that the cautiousness of British European policies was part of their downfall, in particular at the time of the accession negotiation. If only Macmillan had launched his new policy of European integration with more vigour, it is said, he would have been more persuasive and de Gaulle would not have dared to veto British entry into the Common Market. However, politics is the art of the possible, and in view of British and Commonwealth opinon and public sentiments, there is much to be said for Macmillan's attempt to find a way into Europe through the back door. That the door was slammed shut cannot be blamed on Macmillan alone.

NOTES

1. R.P.T. Davenport-Hines, *The Macmillans* (London: Mandarin, 1993), pp. 281.
2. Hansard, House of Commons, 26 November 1956, vol. 561, cols 35–54.
3. *The Messina Resolution.* Adopted by the Ministers of Foreign Affairs of the Member States of the ECSC at their meeting at Messina on 1 and 2 June 1955, White Paper, Cmnd. 9525, July 1955, London, 1955, pp. 7–9, printed in M. Camps, *Britain and the European Community* (Princeton: PUP, 1964), pp. 520–2.
4. H. Macmillan, *Riding the Storm, 1955–1959* (London: Macmillan, 1971) pp. 69.
5. Jebb to FO, 31 May 1955, PRO: FO 371/116038.
6. MAC (55), 15 July 1955, PRO: CAB 134/1026.
7. Minutes in PRO: T 232/431 throughout August 1955. See also M. Dockrill and J.W. Young (eds), *British Foreign Policy 1945–1956* (London: Macmillan, 1989), pp. 197–224 and p. 207.
8. Camps, *Britain and the European Community*, p. 45.
9. MAC (55), 27 October 1955, PRO: CAB 134/1026.
10. For a detailed description of British thinking on Plan G see Macmillan, *Riding the Storm*, pp. 61–88.
11. *Negotiations for a European Free Trade Area. Documents Relating to the Negotiations from July, 1956, to December, 1958*, Cmnd. 641; herein: 'Resolution of the Council of 19th July, 1956, concerning the study of the relations between the proposed European Customs Union and Member countries not taking part therein', C (56) 196, p. 7.
12. Minutes of Cabinet meetings, PRO: CAB 128/30 CC (56) 57 (7), 2 August 1956. CAB papers 191 and 192 of 1956.
13. Hansard, HoC, 26 November 1956, vol. 561, col. 39.

14. For details see R. Bailey, 'Die britische Einstellung zum europäischen Gemeinsamen Markt und zur Freihandelszone', *Europa Archiv*, Vol. 12 (1957), pp. 9803–7.
15. Exports from Commonwealth countries to Great Britain had dropped from 39 per cent in 1938 to 27 per cent in 1956. Commonwealth Economic Committee, *Commonwealth Trade 1950 to 1957* (London, 1959).
16. Between 1938 and 1956 the proportion of exports to the Commonwealth increased from 45 per cent to 49 per cent, that of imports from the Commonwealth from 37 per cent to 45 per cent. Commonwealth Economic Committee, *Commonwealth Trade 1950 to 1957* (London, 1959).
17. W. Wallace, 'After Berrill: Whitehall and the Management of British Diplomacy', *International Affairs*, Vol. 35 (1978), p. 220.
18. CRO (ed.), *The probable development of the Commonwealth over the next 10 or 15 years, and the general political and economic world pattern into which the Commonwealth would satisfactorily fit*, June 1956, PRO: T 234/195.
19. Armstrong (Treasury) for instance remarked in an minute: 'CRO paper gives a slight impression of an attitude, which I have observed elsewhere in the CRO, namely that the Commonwealth is a good thing in itself and that it must be a fundamental objective of policy to keep it in being, without enquiring why this should be so. If this is carried too far we could end up with nothing more than a glossy facade.' Minute Armstrong, 28 June 1956, PRO: T 234/195.
20. Lloyd before the Council of Europe, cited in Camps, *Britain and the European Community*, p. 278.
21. M. Charlton, *The Price of Victory* (London: BBC, 1983), p. 188.
22. R. Lieber, *British Politics and European Unity* (Berkeley: University of California Press, 1970), p. 25.
23. Camps, *Britain and the European Community*, pp. 509. See also D.C. Watt, 'Großbritannien und Europa. 1951–1959. Die Jahre konservativer Regierung', *Vierteljahreshefte für Zeitgeschichte*, Vol. 28 (1980), pp. 398–409.
24. See G. Crowther, 'Reconstruction of an Alliance', *Foreign Affairs*, Vol. 35 (1957), pp. 173–83.
25. *Picture Post*, 28 October 1939, quoted in H. Macmillan, *Tides of Fortune, 1945–1955* (London: Macmillan, 1969), p. 152.
26. Macmillan, *Tides of Fortune*, pp. 181–3.
27. R. Bullen and M.E. Pelly (eds), *Documents of British Policy Overseas*, Series II, Vol. 1, No. 155 (London: HMSO, 1986), pp. 286–7.
28. See also: 'Europe: Federal or Confederal', in Macmillan, *Tides of Fortune*, pp. 185–227.
29. For a list of meetings of the MAC see: PRO: T 234/195–206.
30. Brook to Macmillan, 1959, PRO: PREM 11/2912.
31. Shuckburgh about Eden's European policy, in Charlton, *The Price of Victory*, p. 172.

32. Charlton, *The Price of Victory*, p. 176.
33. Macmillan, *Riding the Storm* p. 69.
34. PRO: CAB 128/26, CC 19 (55), 30 June 1955. Bearing this in mind, it seems rather doubtful whether Wolfram Kaiser's celebration of Macmillan's 'liberation' from his 'European halo' (*Frankfurter Allgemeine Zeitung*, 19 August 1992) is justified and whether his turn to Europe was really an 'alternativlose Flucht aus einer innen- und außenpolitischen Sackgasse, die alles andere als eine Neuorientierung bedeutete' (flight out of a foreign political and domestic dead-end without alternatives, which was anything but a new orientation).
35. Charlton, *The Price of Victory*, p. 194.
36. Charlton, *The Price of Victory*, pp. 184–5.
37. H.J. Küsters, *Die Gründung der Europäischen Gemeinschaft* (Baden-Baden: Nomos, 1982), pp. 280–321.
38. The most uncertain factor in the EEC discussions in autumn and winter 1956–57 was France. In German diplomatic circles it was judged that the German reaction to the Suez Crisis caused the decisive turn in French policies towards European integration (private information). The definite 'yes' of the French delegation to the Common Market followed in January 1957. Küster, *Die Gründung der Europäischen Gemeinschaft*, pp. 419–22.
39. Charlton, *The Price of Victory*, pp. 237.
40. FO minute, 10 June 1959, PRO: FO 371/143702.
41. N. Beloff, *Transit of Britain* (London, 1973), p. 172.
42. Minute P.H. Gore-Booth for Foreign Secretary, 8 July 1960, PRO: FO 371/150362.
43. ES(E)(60), 25 May 1960, PRO: CAB 134/1852.
44. The United Kingdom and the European Economic Community, 8 July 1960, PRO: FO 371/150362.
45. J. Moon, *European Integration in British Politics: A Study of Change* (Aldershot: Gower, 1985), p. 162.
46. Moon, *European Integration in British Politics*, p. 163.
47. N. Beloff, *The General Says No* (Harmondsworth: Penguin, 1963), pp. 108.
48. H. Macmillan, *At the End of the Day, 1959–1961* (London: Macmillan, 1973), p. 16.
49. Beloff, *The General Says No*, p. 110.

7 'Staying in the Game': Harold Macmillan and Britain's World Role

Richard Aldous and Sabine Lee

When Harold Macmillan resigned from office in 1963, his public reputation as the elegant and unflappable 'Supermac' had been tarnished by scandal and apparent incompetence. It took more than two decades for that reputation to recover when, as Lord Stockton, he was acclaimed on his return to the British political stage, now equipped, in Lord Jenkin's words, with 'the essential appurtenances of venerable sagacity and elderly wit'. When he died in 1986, *The Times* hailed him as Disraeli's true heir, commenting that 'both men combined the radical and the traditional in their politics and thus were able to persuade Conservative parties to carry through far reaching changes of policy at home and abroad.'

Macmillan, like Disraeli, had a penchant for self-aggrandisement and recognised the importance of image in politics. He took acting lessons from the comedian Bud Flanagan and perfected a routine for every occasion based on his early experiences. Lofty aristocrat and crofter's grandson, heroic veteran of the First World War and contemplative scholar – he could, and did, play them all. Elegant, witty and unflappable, with his Old Etonian tie and Balliol shuffle, he seemed to many the very model of an Edwardian gentleman. But behind Macmillan's clubbability and elegant wit lay great personal unhappiness. Macmillan, like his hero, Churchill, suffered appalling 'black dog' depressions and could never escape 'the inside feeling that something awful and unknown was about to happen'. When these 'black dog' moods came during the premiership, Rab Butler, his deputy, would 'step in and take over the Cabinet', insisting that Macmillan 'go away for a few days' to read Jane Austen and recover his emotional balance.

Macmillan's fatalism caused him personal distress but it was also his spur to 'greatness'. He was driven by a sense that he was destined to be Churchill's true heir and believed his place in history would be determined by his performance on the world stage. International affairs dominated his thoughts whilst in office and he sought to maintain a firm grip on Britain's foreign policy. He surprised commentators and politicians in 1957 by keeping Selwyn Lloyd, humiliated by the Suez crisis, at the Foreign Office as a lame-duck Secretary of State. Nine months after a stunning electoral victory in the autumn of 1959, he replaced Lloyd with Lord Home, a more skilful and imaginative minister, but handicapped by his exclusion from the House of Commons. Skilful placement ensured that Macmillan, like his predecessors Churchill and Eden, remained at centre stage in foreign affairs and guaranteed his pre-eminence in establishing the foreign policy agenda.

Macmillan's unquestionable ascendancy in foreign policy was facilitated by the array of talents with which he surrounded himself at No. 10. His private secretaries, Freddie Bishop and Philip de Zulueta, were young, bright and unconventional in their thinking, and ultimately sacrificed their high-flying careers in order to serve Macmillan beyond the call of duty. In particular, de Zulueta, with special responsibility for foreign affairs, exposed Macmillan to ideas that had not been dulled by the relentless need for referral and redrafting that often afflicts bureaucratic organisations like the Foreign Office. Evidence of de Zulueta's role as a 'player' in policy debates is clear from his perceptive and elegant minutes to the Prime Minister debunking advice from King Charles Street and reproduced as minutes from the Prime Minister himself. It was hardly surprising that Selwyn Lloyd should have protested to de Zulueta and Bishop of 'government by private secretary', but indicative of the pair's confidence in their patronage that their tart reply was: 'Well, the only alternative is government by politician.'

In control of the broad foreign policy agenda and surrounded by able advisers, Macmillan was well placed to implement his ideas about Britain's world role. Macmillan was, by repute, a great thinker, and he thought of himself as Britain's best read Prime Minister. Sir Frederick Bishop, commenting in *The Times* for the centenary of Macmillan's birth, observed that his 'view of both national and international politics was always strategic, based on his own deep reading of history.' Certainly, Macmillan was always ready with an appropriate historical analogy for contemporary world events, but what aside from casual one-liners is the basis of his reputation as a great thinker and strategist? Clearly, it is not his published work. He made little contribution to literature or historical writing, particularly when compared with his role model, Churchill. His own multi-volumed memoirs are thought by most to be verbose and, as a read, surprisingly dull. A comparison with the memoirs of his contemporary, Charles de Gaulle, highlights a certain lack of rigour on Macmillan's part and an apparently superficial understanding of the politics of the age. Only his *War Diaries* provide original insight although it seems likely that his most incisive contribution will come when, eventually, his personal diaries are published.

If Macmillan's published historical reflections are of mixed quality, his reputation as a strategist must rest on his political thinking whilst in office. Alistair Horne, Macmillan's official biographer, believes that Macmillan had 'underneath the often flippant exterior, a most penetrating mind, which asked all the key questions of our times.' When he became Prime Minister in 1957, Britain had reached something of a strategic crossroad, a time when 'key questions needed not just to be asked but answered.

Since the Second World War, Britain had faced a dilemma about the political and economic implications of its diminishing world role; the Suez Crisis had symbolised the inability of British policy-makers to address the complex issues involved with anything approaching a coherent, modern strategy. Strategic 'overstretch' and a misguided attempt to maintain influence in all three of Churchill's 'circles' – Europe, Commonwealth and the 'special relation-ship' – had driven Britain to the wall economically. Britain had retained the vestiges of global power and was on the verge of exploding a thermonuclear bomb, but it was clear that strategic priorities had to be put into sharper focus if the vestiges of great power status were to be preserved.

Macmillan, to his great credit, had been one of the few politicians to recognise this fact during the early 1950s. 'It is no longer the case of chosing between the policies of Marlborough and Bolingbroke,' he declared to Churchill in suitably historical terms, 'but of combining them.' Less pro-saically, he argued that 'external expenditure [has] broken our backs', believing that the instincts that encouraged Britain to maintain a global role had to be constrained by economic reality. 'The old concept of national self-sufficiency is out of date,' the new Prime Minister told Cabinet in 1957. 'The countries of the free world can maintain their security only by combining their resources and sharing their tasks.'

The essays in this collection demonstrate Macmillan's willingness to 'think big' and rise above the minutiae of day-to-day politics in order to question priorities. But it is also clear that Macmillan retained a traditional understanding about Britain's role in world politics and, like his predeces-sors, believed that Britain still had a world role to preserve.

Past glories dominated his perception of the country's position causing him to exaggerate Britain's power and in-dependence. As a consequence, he underestimated the rel-ative strength of Britain's partners, and, along with many of his Cabinet colleagues, misconceived the extent to which the United States and the European allies were prepared to take into account British views when formulating their own policies. It was this attitude that had led Anthony Eden into the adventure at Suez and now contributed to Macmillan's miscalculation of British bargaining strength in most spheres of foreign policy.

Macmillan's illusions of British grandeur were at their most transparent in early 1959. With the chief play-maker of

Western strategy, John Foster Dulles, fatally ill, Macmillan set out to fill the vacuum in American foreign policy and take East–West relations into his (as he believed) capable and powerful hands. The pseudo-independent policy he pursued between 1959 and 1960, symbolised by the Moscow visit (February/March 1959), and clearly evident during the Geneva Foreign Ministers' Meeting (April 1959), Paris Western Summit (December 1959) and Paris Summit (May 1960), did not enhance British international prestige but succeeded only in alienating partners within the Western Alliance. The British desire to run an independent show, with a minimum of consultation, had a detrimental effect on bilateral relations and cohesion within the Western camp. Britain's relations with Germany and France, which were both inherently suspicious of British reliability, and America, which was less suspicious, all suffered as a result of Macmillan's attempts at carrying out an autonomous policy.

The limitations on Britain executing a genuinely independent role have been demonstrated in each of the essays collected here. They are most evident in Macmillan's Moscow visit in early 1959. Even though he and his Foreign Secretary, Selwyn Lloyd, offered concessions and showed great flexibility in secret talks with their Soviet counterparts, they could not have carried through any such concessions without the approval of the United States, France or even Germany. Hence, the British insistence that the visit was not one of negotiation, but only of discussion, was a political necessity and not a tactical choice.

Macmillan's negotiations in the context of European co-operation and integration showed similar misconceptions. Macmillan was a European in the sense that he wanted Britain linked to the continent in a way that served Britain's position at the centre of the 'three circles'. But in the European race Britain, and to an extent Macmillan himself, had lagged behind from the outset. When Macmillan realised that the group of countries setting the pace of integration had decided for a fast race, the British, despite increasing their own speed significantly, could no longer catch up. By 1963 it had become clear that Britain's reorientation towards Europe had foundered not so much on doing too little by way of concessions as doing it too late. Again, Macmillan had overestimated British bargaining power, especially at times when the British had to compete with the French for German support, as in the decisive phases of the free trade area negotiations or the EEC accession negotiations. The intensity of the Franco-German reconciliation and understanding achieved by Adenauer and de Gaulle was hardly predictable in 1958, yet a certain lack of realism was a consistent feature of the British assessment of their own position in international affairs. Facts and figures which pointed at the limitations of British strength were disregarded or explained away, and past rather than present power realities pushed to the front of self-perception.

If the British were slow to react to changes in the shift of the European power balance, change in defence policy was equally sluggish. Even the British 1957 Defence White Paper, which was hailed by the government as the most profound change in military strategy of normal times, could not reverse the general trend in British defence policy towards preserving Britain's world role. Britain wanted to stay in the power game with a global military role, despite a poverty of economic resources. Recognition of economic limitations only fuelled discussions of *how* Britain's global role could be preserved – not *whether* it could, or should, be retained at all.

Middle Eastern as well as colonial policies followed a similar pattern. The prime concern remained how to maintain national power: in the former case by military presence in the area to preserve economic interest, notably access to oil, and, in the latter case by strengthening Commonwealth links whilst withdrawing from the colonies. Nowhere was this more obvious than in Macmillan's Commonwealth tours in 1958 and 1960 which helped him emphasise his role as a world statesman and, by implication, the continuing stature of Britain on the world stage. The loss of prestige and a practical power base which accompanied the 'winds of change' was an unexpected and unwelcome side-effect of that process, which, like the Defence White Paper, had been a conscious attempt to shore-up Britain's world role.

In all these areas, Macmillan was the unquestioned master of the British agenda. Like the German Chancellor, Konrad Adenauer, he did not trust his colleagues to run foreign policy effectively and sensibly, and was convinced that heads of government should make the decisions on which would depend the preservation of world peace. Macmillan's personal diplomacy, however, shows time after time a misjudgement of other leaders in Western Europe, the United States and the Soviet Union. He believed that he could transform Khrushchev's policy of confrontation over Berlin into cooperation and thereby save the world from war, but he was humiliated by the Soviet Premier. He set out to use his 'influence' on Adenauer to neutralise de Gaulle's antagonism towards a more involved British role in Europe without recognising that the French President's impact on the Chancellor far surpassed his own. He embarked on a mission to secure East–West *détente* by summitry only to watch his hopes disintegrate at the shambolic Paris Summit. He fostered good personal relations with successive American Presidents in order to preserve the 'special relationship' without recognising that the partnership was generally interpreted as British servility towards Washington.

Yet Macmillan's management of British affairs was not without its successes. His policy objectives may not have come to fruition during his term as Prime Minister but they did set down the political agenda for British policy until at least 1979.

The essays collected here have demonstrated Macmillan's skill at handling the Cabinet and show an instinctive feel about when to be cautious or radical, not least in making ministerial appointments. In 1957, he refrained from sacrificing the obvious Suez scapegoat, Selwyn Lloyd, in order to keep a firm grip on foreign affairs, and he retained Alan Lennox-Boyd as a no-risk Colonial Secretary. But when Macmillan felt ready to confront a particular issue, caution was abandoned and 'believers' were installed to carry through his agenda in the face of bureaucratic and political opposition. After the 1959 general election, Lennox-Boyd was replaced as Colonial Secretary by the young Iain Macleod in what proved a timely strategic decision. He successfully engineered the British retreat from Africa while managing to sell it to the British public as a noble yet strategically deft operation. In the defence sector, Macmillan appointed Duncan Sandys to overhaul the military. He was a notoriously stubborn minister, well-equipped to survive the bitter fights with the three services and prepared to take the inevitable flak in order to push unpopular decisions through the Cabinet and Parliament. On the European platform, key ministerial positions were filled by colleagues who shared his belief that Britain's place was at the centre of Europe rather than on the periphery. Macmillan appointed the fiercely loyal Chief Whip, Edward Heath, as Lord Privy Seal to negotiate Britain into the EEC and ensured that ministries such as Agriculture, Fisheries and Food were in the hands of staunch pro-Europeans. They helped to convince both the Cabinet and the public that Britain had to move closer to continental Europe and, eventually, aim at membership of the EEC. Until 1961, the public had been told consistently that Britain could not join the Common Market because of its obligations to the Commonwealth. It is one of Macmillan's great achievements that he was able to persuade the Conservative Party and the country as a whole that Britain's course had to be changed. Macmillan failed in his bid to lead Britain into the EEC and had to wait another decade to see the country finally win membership. But it had been his shift in policy that had pushed Britain in the right direction and paved the way for the removal of the remaining obstacles to British entry during the late 1960s.

Critics have accused Harold Macmillan of a lack of consistency in his foreign policy strategy, some even denying that he had a strategy at all. Priorities in his political agenda appeared to shift without any obvious sense of direction and, at first sight, it is difficult to detect a consistent overarching design in this pattern. Closer inspection, however, reveals a central theme running through Macmillan's strategy, deeply rooted in his own personality.

Harold Macmillan was convinced about his vocation as a world leader. Not only did he want to go down in history as a fine statesman and great peacemaker of the twentieth century (and in this he was no different from his contemporaries on the world stage), he was also convinced that he had a special duty to fulfil this role. His sense of responsibility before mankind had its root in his need to pay tribute to those who had lost their lives in the trenches at the Western Front during the First World War. The lasting effect of the Great War on Macmillan can hardly be overestimated. The apparently senseless loss of young lives which he witnessed during those years helps to explain why international security and the avoidance of war should have remained the constant feature of his thinking on foreign policy.

In the light of ever more powerful weapons of mass destruction Macmillan considered the preservation of peace as the most important political task. There were very few issues which he considered worth fighting over militarily: not the colonies, not Berlin, and certainly not German unity. The Prime Minister's search for lasting peace was at the core of his policy of 'negotiation at all costs' with the Soviets in 1959 after the Berlin ultimatum, his emphasis on summitry and his persistence on the issue of a nuclear test ban treaty in the early 1960s. Even his European policy fits into this pattern. Macmillan had actively supported European integration in the immediate postwar years as a means of bringing Germany firmly into the Western Alliance system. When the 1960 Paris Summit collapsed taking down with it his vision of East–West *détente*, Macmillan returned to Europe at least partly as a means to securing international security.

It is unlikely that, as *The Independent* claimed on his death, Harold Macmillan will be remembered as Britain's 'most successful postwar Prime Minister', but the 'real' Macmillan remains somewhat elusive. The political commentator Malcolm Muggeridge once observed that in successful administrations the Cabinet was divided into priests and bookies: the priests to provide the spiritual uplifts and the bookies to tell the jokes. To many of his contemporaries, Macmillan seemed to combine the characteristics of both professions, managing, in the words of Lord Wilson of Rievaulx, to be 'great fun and absolutely dead serious'. Harold Macmillan's abilities as a 'bookie' are well known. As Sir Robert Rhodes James remembers in his opening essay to this collection, when Macmillan became Prime Minister, 'every one cheered up'.

And yet, beneath the bookie's facade, there was something of a priest about Macmillan. He would often appeal to the moral highground in debate, particularly in discussions about war, urging cynical colleagues to remember 'our duty to God and to Mankind'. Many doubted the genuineness of his moral outburst arguing, like Eisenhower, that it was 'just an act he put on'. But even though Macmillan loved playing to the crowd and devoted considerable attention to his image, there can be little doubting his genuine sense of duty as a survivor of the Great War 'to make some decent use of the life that had been spared'.

Index

159